RICHARD DEMARCO, now aged 94, has had what he calls 'The Real Scotland' and 'The an outward looking Scotland mercifully dis inherently disingenuous agendas of the co... ....ou..u. What Demarco means by this is his engagement through education, theatre and the arts with the enduring personalities, edifices, old landed estates, and entrenched cultural antiquities which are at the core of Scotland's European history. This is the Scotland of the Demarco Gallery, the Richard Demarco Archive, and the Friends of Richard Demarco, living and dead, scattered throughout the world, each and every one of them embodying the Soul of Scotland. For these are the influences that have created Scotland's European art landscape and forged the potent historical sweep of the dialogue we all like to think we cherish but far too often choose to disregard.

RODDY MARTINE, as writer, historian and past editor of *Scottish Field*, *Scottish Life*, *Scotland Magazine* and *The Keeper*, and contributor to *Scottish Quest* magazine, *The Scotsman*, *The Herald*, *Edinburgh Evening News* and *Scottish Daily Mail*, has, over 60 years, written extensively on the global reach of the Scots.

Demarco's Scotland

RICHARD DEMARCO and RODDY MARTINE

Richard Demarco (signature)

Luath Press Limited

EDINBURGH

www.luath.co.uk

*This book is dedicated to the memory of Ronald Craig,
art master at Glenalmond College 1956–1987
and a friend and fellow artist-teacher of Richard Demarco*

First published 2024

ISBN: 978-1-80425-166-9

The paper used in this book is recyclable It is made from low-chlorine pulps
produced in a low-energy, low-emission manner from renewable forests

FSC
www.fsc.org
FSC® C023367

The mark of
responsible forestry

Printed and bound by
Robertson Printers, Forfar

Typeset in 11.5 point Sabon by
Main Point Books, Edinburgh

Contents

Introduction

The question arose at a *Demarco's Edinburgh* book talk chaired by Jackie McGlone at the Royal Scots Club in Edinburgh on 23 November 2023. The authors' response was unequivocal.

Following the astonishing triumph of that first Edinburgh International Festival of Music and the Arts in 1947, the twin messages of post-war reconciliation and the healing balm of multiculturalism remained starkly manifest, at least for a while.

In his townhouse art gallery in the West End of Edinburgh's New Town, the Italo-Celt Richard Demarco, Edinburgh born and bred, teacher and accomplished artist, had by then come to the conclusion that an annual three-week programme of music, theatre, dance and the visual arts was simply not enough.

'You can either be a tourist in the Art World, or an explorer,' observed Dore Ashton, doyenne of New York's international art critics. Exploration was therefore the name of the game; humankind's endless quest for the shock of the new.

With Edinburgh's creative roots so deeply embedded in the cultural traditions of Europe, and the New World, Richard Demarco was convinced Scotland had so much more to offer. 'Scotland deserves a 12 month festival,' he announced. Thus under the auspices of the Demarco Gallery and Edinburgh University, the first EDINBURGH ARTS Summer School was launched in 1972, increasing momentum in all of the decades that followed.

Richard Demarco believes life should always be a celebration of ALL THE ARTS, including science, blended into a fusion of creativity and love. Taking the lead from his friend, the German-born Joseph Beuys, those EDINBURGH ARTS journeys into Scotland's hinterland and beyond into Europe were, in all of their enthralling and conflicting diversity, simply an exploration of the history of ideas. Those ideas all have their origins in the tentacles of Continental Europe.

Engagingly confrontational, driven by a life-force of deeply embedded passion, the first domiciled UK citizen to be awarded the

European Citizen medal by the European Parliament in Brussels, remains intransigent.

Diversity and originality. Add on to these the physical localities and cast of characters from those EDINBURGH ARTS explorations over seven decades and you have the core of Demarco's narrative.

What are you all doing here? All of Scotland's artistic and self determination emanates from two millenniums of cultural interaction with Continental Europe.

Thus came about the Scottish play performed in Belarusian on the battlements of Ravenscraig Castle; the introduction of Joseph Beuys to the Rannoch Moor to inspire the planting of 7,000 oak trees; John Osborne's play *Look Back in Anger* spoken in Italian; a 1917 Spanish-built polacca-rigged brig exploring the Inner Hebrides; light show projection onto the walls of Torness Nuclear Power Station; the introduction of Scotland to the Venice Biennale; William Shakespeare's *Romeo & Juliet* enacted at Craigmillar Castle, and the search for Ossian in the Sound of Sleat.

Those who have known Richard Demarco over the decades will be aware that he is rarely seen in public without a camera around his neck, busily taking photographs of those around him even when he is himself being interviewed on camera. At first it was an Instamatic with film, then a digital device to the extent that there are now several million images in the Richard Demarco Archive, a remarkable record of those he has known and the places he has visited and influenced throughout his remarkable career. As such, readers of *Demarco's Scotland* are invited to approach the following chapters not as a natural progression of location and text but as a series of vignettes from the life and times of a charismatic individual whose impact on the cultural reputation of Scotland is unsurpassed.

These are but a handful of the heartbeats and footprints that have engaged Richard Demarco in his journey through life and inspired his multitude of admirers, making possible his 94 pioneering years and still counting.

Nobody could surely ever accuse Richard Demarco CBE of being boring.

Roddy Martine, Edinburgh,
July 2024

Prologue

I MUST BE forever grateful to Richard Noyce. It was he who invited me in 1983 to speak on a lecture tour that he organised for me to make contact with the world in which he had found himself gainfully employed, in the cultural life developed in and around the Newbury Art Centre in south-west England.

My lecture tour took me to Southampton College of Art and it was there that I met Terry Ann Newman, a student studying painting and sculpture. In 1985, I invited her to join my EDINBURGH ARTS expedition to the Dorset world of Jonathan Phipps which was centred on his concept of a unique sculpture park in Tout Quarry on the Isle of Portland. Terry Newman then decided to participate in the two EDINBURGH ARTS expeditions which followed shortly afterwards.

Her discovery, in 1986, of the Polish art world proved to be a source of inspiration to her career as an artist; so much so that, on the death in 1998 of her husband John Newman at the tragically early age of 59, she decided the following year to move to Edinburgh to help explore the world of EDINBURGH ARTS and, in so doing, help to develop the Demarco Archive and in particular that vitally important part which was not purchased by the Scottish National Gallery of Modern Art in 1995.

I consider that at the heart of the Demarco Archive is my personal experience of each and every one of the Edinburgh Festival programmes from the inaugural programmes of the official Edinburgh International Festival conjoined with that of the Edinburgh Festival Fringe. For me, they are inseparably part of the curtain going up and coming down over the three weeks when Edinburgh is no longer the capital of Scotland, but the world capital of culture. It should be noted that the first event marking the birth of 'The Fringe' took place, not in Edinburgh but in the Romanesque cathedral of Dunfermline with a production of *Everyman*, the medieval morality play. This historical play has always inspired me to contribute to both the official and Fringe programmes. It is my firm belief that the international festival spirit should enhance those parts of Scotland well beyond the city boundaries of Edinburgh to all over Scotland and further to all of the British Isles to encompass the European Continent and world culture.

I regarded myself and all my fellow Festival-goers as cultural pilgrims who travelled the length and breadth of Europe towards the shrine of Saint Andrew in the Cathedral of St Andrews, marking his martyrdom, second only to the Basilica of Saint Peter, his brother, in Rome, and fellow Christian martyr.

More often than not, the medieval pilgrim routes followed those of the farmers as cattle and sheep drovers. These historic drovers' roads were also used by medieval scholars and students, linking Scotland's universities with those of Europe. I recognised these ancient byways as more important than 20th-century motorways and any road system that does not obscure the lie of the land – immemorable landscape known to our prehistoric European ancestors. 'Meikle Seggie' is the name of a farm in the Ochil Hills, marking the foothills of the Grampian Mountains. My father spent his youth nearby in this landscape in the small Fifeshire town of Kelty.

However, his Demarco family Italian ancestors came from the Italian equivalent of the Grampians – the Apennine Mountains between Rome and Naples. The Demarco family were part of a historic farming community and, indeed, were famous as shepherds. It was as such, as Italian peasants, that they made their way, often in penury, on foot from near to Monte Cassino towards the Wall of the Emperor Antoninus Pius, marking the north-west extremity of the Roman Empire in the Celtic Kingdom of Dalriada, linking the estuaries of the Rivers Forth and Clyde.

Meikle Seggie is the road from farmscape to the cityscape of Edinburgh. For me, therefore, the journey of the Festival-goer or artistic practitioner begins on the road leading to Edinburgh and especially the nodal points of these roads identified as points marking artistic endeavour forever blessed by the art of the *Book of Kells* and the sacred island of Iona, the studios of Margot Sandeman on the Isle of Arran and her studio and garden in Bearsden.

The Road to Meikle Seggie is of significance to my history of the Edinburgh Festival because it entwines the Festival's history with that of Scotland itself as well as the history of Edinburgh. This year of 2024 is of particular significance because it celebrates the 900th anniversary of Edinburgh's City status. Surely, the Edinburgh Festival, in its 77th year of existence, must acknowledge this historic fact.

Roddy Martine, as the co-writer to this sequel to the Luath Press publication *Demarco's Edinburgh*, has focused his contribution on key nodal points that he has selected on 'The Road to Meikle Seggie'. His contribution, therefore, consists of a series of essays. The titles of each essay has given me nourishing food for thought.

The title of this book can be understood in the form of a question – 'What on earth are you doing here?' This is the question I addressed to the audience who gathered in Edinburgh's Royal Scots Club towards the end of last year. They had listened to the conversation that Roddy Martine and I had enjoyed, reminiscing on our co-authorship of *Demarco's Edinburgh*, aided by the insightful chairmanship of the writer and journalist Jackie McGlone.

Roddy Martine has added a subtitle to this sequel – 'Richard Demarco's battle for the Soul of Scotland'. The battle began in 1947 when I experienced the first Edinburgh Festival. I realised even then that Edinburgh had been both blessed and challenged to the breaking point when it was transformed from being Scotland's capital city to the world's Capital of Culture, as an expression of 'the flowering of the human spirit' in the aftermath of the suffering endured by humanity during the Second World War.

Roddy Martine's first essay is entitled 'Meikle Seggie Forever'. This essay is a well-nigh perfect introduction to the sequel because it is focused on how I somehow, almost miraculously, found myself among countless friends as a schoolboy at Edinburgh's one and only secondary school offering a Roman Catholic education. I learned that my allegiance was not to the British Empire but to the concept of Christendom and to the Christo-Judaic dynamic wedded to that of the Greco-Romano. In my Roman Catholic parish church of St John's Portobello, and in the Roman Catholic Cathedral of St Mary's, I learned to pray and sing in Latin and discovered the pre-Reformation music of Robert Carver and the poetry of Robert Henryson and William Dunbar.

My concept of The Road to Meikle Seggie identified Edinburgh as a distinctly European city by the Gothic and medieval architecture of its Old Town and the Italianate architecture identified with its New Town designed on Palladian rules. Pre-Reformation Edinburgh was possessed of distinctly Roman Catholic religious sites in the Church of The Holy Trinity, in the spire of St Giles' Cathedral shaped as the crown of Charlemagne, Emperor of Europe, and in the walls of St Margaret's Chapel on Edinburgh's Castle Hill protected by the surrounding battlements of Edinburgh Castle, the place of pilgrimage and the burial place of Scotland's Stuart Kings within the sad ruins of Holyrood Abbey and its surrounding landscapes as a place of medieval refuge.

EDINBURGH ARTS transformed the Richard Demarco Gallery at 8 Melville Crescent into a 'University of ALL the Arts', in collaboration with Edinburgh University's Schools of Scottish and Extra-Mural Studies centred on Edinburgh University's George Square and the 18th-century interior of St Cecilia's Hall, as well as in Lochgilphead High School and the Valley of Kilmartin in Argyll. Kilmartin is the Gaelic name for Saint Martin of Tours, the Roman martyr. He was an inspiration to Saint Columba. That is why the Provençal Roman world of this Roman soldier is identified with the majestic Celtic cross standing proudly to this day to greet pilgrims on the ancient road to Iona Abbey. I regard this ancient road as a distinctly Christian section of The Road to Meikle Seggie, linking Scotland's Hebridean world with that of the Mediterranean shoreline of Provence.

Roddy Martine has wisely entitled his second essay thus: 'But first you have to know your European history'. In order to bring that history firmly placed into the 20th century, I have never forgotten that, without the tragedy of the Second World War, the Edinburgh Festival would never have come into existence in the lifetime of a German-speaking Austrian refugee who sought refuge in 1932 in Britain from Hitler's Nazi Germany – to find himself in the safe haven of the Christie family in their West Sussex house of Glyndebourne. As the former pre-war director of Europe's historic opera festival in Salzburg, Rudolf Bing became the founding director of the now world-famous Glyndebourne Opera.

Eva, the Countess of Rosebery, was a loyal supporter of Glyndebourne, even though she lived in Dalmeny House on her Dalmeny Estate and Edinburgh did not have an airport. The 500-mile road or rail journey was tedious. It could be said that the meetings at Dalmeny House between Lady Rosebery and her opera-loving friends gave birth to the Edinburgh Festival.

I myself fell in love with opera through the sound of my father's bel canto tenor singing of excerpts from opera in Italian, together with his sister Cristina's son Umberto. Umberto Demarco had been trained in Italy by the world-renowned Italian opera singer Beniamino Gigli. His promising career began with his debut performance in Edinburgh's Usher Hall. Sadly, his career did not materialise because of Mussolini's decision to have Italy with its Fascist government as an ally of Nazi Germany.

However, Rudolf Bing, as the Edinburgh International Festival's founding director, made sure that for its first three years of existence, the Edinburgh Festival expressed the spirit of both the festivals of Salzburg and Glyndebourne.

Roddy Martine's third essay is entitled 'All in the Mind's Eye'. I am personally grateful to him for emphasising the fact that I am essentially a visual artist who studied at Edinburgh College of Art's Design School and the processes of printmaking, book illustration, book publication, mural painting, life drawing and painting. I therefore regarded the artists I exhibited at The Traverse Art Gallery and later at the Richard Demarco Gallery as 'fellow artists'.

I never regarded myself as a gallery director. The Traverse Gallery was born in my art room at Scotus Academy. I regarded myself as an artist-teacher – as a teacher using art language. I was reassured that this was an edifying role when, in 1970, I asked Joseph Beuys 'What is the essential nature of your art?'

His answer was simple and direct – 'My art is my teaching'. That is why many of the master works that he made in Scotland were made as white chalk drawings on blackboards. I personally regarded my work as a 20th-century artist as a sculptural installation. I realised that it was my responsibility to transform it into such a complete artistic statement – not as a display of art works independent of each other. As a complete exhibition, they possessed a powerful statement. I was always saddened by the thought that this artistic entity would be fragmented and dismantled by the processes of selling individual art works.

Roddy Martine's subsequent essays provide the backdrop to my Collision Course with the Scottish Arts Council, a confrontation which changed my life and directly influenced the paths that I was to follow in the years thereafter.

I knew I could not have expected the Scottish Arts Council to support the academic roles I gladly accepted from Kingston University throughout the decade of the Nineties, first of all as a Stanley Picker Fellow and later as the University's Professor of European Cultural Studies under the patronage of and in collaboration with Kingston's Professor David Youlton. These academic roles enabled me to strengthen the cultural dialogues I had already established in the Sixties and Seventies, in particular with Poland, Romania, Hungary and the former Yugoslavia – all imprisoned by the Soviet Communist empire behind Josef Stalin's Iron Curtain.

Lord Kames, one of the luminaries of the Scottish Enlightenment, famously stated 'All the arts, whether expressed in literature, the performing and visual arts, are perfectly acceptable. However, surely that which is the most important is that of agriculture.'

I was heartened by this controversial statement and it led me to accept the offer I received by a telephone call from Johnny Watson, an East Lothian farmer, in response to a BBC Radio programme. I was interviewed by Zevi Watmough and I am forever grateful to her for enabling me to make a plea to BBC Radio prime-time listeners that I needed a space large enough to exhibit the large-scale nature of the Demarco Archive under my direction since 1995 when the Scottish National Gallery of Modern Art had acquired part of it.

Johnny Watson's farm was located dramatically beside the Torness Nuclear Power Station on a stretch of arable farmland associated with the boyhood of John Muir who acquired world-renown as the creator of the concept of national parks. Naturally, I gratefully accepted this inspiring offer. I had long been aware of the historic importance of the North Sea coastline south of Edinburgh, leading to the English border town of Berwick-upon-Tweed. It is encircled by late Renaissance defensive walls reminiscent of those who built the Italian city of Lucca, in close proximity to the medieval town of Barga which is proudly known as the most Scottish town in Tuscany.

Barga is twinned to the East Lothian fishing port of Port Seton due entirely to the life and art of John Bellany, the acclaimed Scottish painter who, through his paintings, created an enduring Scottish–Italian cultural dialogue.

Another Scottish–Italian cultural dialogue is associated with the historic East Lothian harbour of Dunbar. There, in 1435, Aeneas Piccolomini was grateful to have found a safe haven from a violent storm at sea which threatened his mission as a Papal Legate to the Court of King James 1. Knowing that his life had been spared, he went on a pilgrimage to a nearby important place of pilgrimage within the walls of what was known as Whitekirk. This church still stands, as does the medieval building in which pilgrims found welcome rest. Aeneas Piccolomini later became Pope Pius the Second, providing ample proof that Scotland played an important part in the Europe of Christendom.

Divine Intervention did indeed cause King David 1 to create a royal pilgrimage route from his mother's chapel encircled by its Edinburgh Castle walls down to the abbey that he built protecting the High Altar marking the spot where he encountered the legendary 'White Stag' with its flaming Cross between its antlers. Beside it now stands the royal residence of the Palace of Holyroodhouse, first named as the Holy Rude or Holy Cross. One mile separates St Margaret's Chapel and Holyrood Abbey. It is, indeed, a Royal Mile – and on it the Edinburgh Festival Fringe was born as well as the Traverse Theatre Club which was born in 1963 out of Cambridge University's Sphynx Club in the Royal Mile's Lawnmarket.

Over the 30 years since 1995, the history of the Edinburgh Festival has been brought thoroughly up-to-date encapsulated within the history of the Demarco Archive as a REAL Artwork.

During this period, the Edinburgh Festival has been under the direction of four directors. The first of these was Sir Brian McMaster whose 16 years overlong directorship ended in 2006. He was succeeded by Sir Jonathan Mills in 2007 who almost immediately invited me to present an exhibition of the Demarco Archive together with a 21-day long lecture programme in the prestigious festival venue of The Scottish National Portrait Gallery.

Unfortunately, that ended my involvement in the Edinburgh Festival's Official Programme because of Sir Brian MacMaster's decision that the Official Festival Programme would well do without the Visual Arts. Sadly, to this day this decision has held firm during the directorships of Fergus Linehan and Nicola Benedetti.

From 1995 to 2000, the first year of the Third Millennium, I benefited from my association with Kingston University, perhaps the most significant five-year period when as Kingston's Stanley Picker

Fellow and later as Kingston's Professor of European Cultural Studies, I involved the history of Scotland with that of the European Youth Parliament sessions in the Reichstag in Berlin, at Oxford University, and for the Scotland House within the European Parliament in Brussells. With an exhibition and symposium entitled *Scotland In Europe: Europe In Scotland.*

It should not be forgotten that in the year 2010, the Demarco Archive attracted financial support directly from the Scottish Government; also from the governments of Germany, Poland, Romania and Serbia.

And that the Scottish Parliament of Holyrood was involved in a cross-party motion presented by Linda Fabiani MSP to the Minister of Culture Fiona Hyslop MSP. After a two-hour parliamentary session at which all parties were represented by speakers pre-empting a celebration of my 80th birthday, Fiona Hyslop announced that the Scottish Government would celebrate my 80th birthday with an exhibition together with a one-day symposium in the Scotland House of the European Parliament in Brussels entitled 'Scotland in Europe: Europe in Scotland.'

Sandy Moffat OBE, as a senior Royal Scottish Academician was appointed Exhibition Co-ordinator, and Fiona Hyslop attended the exhibition. It should be noted that this was the second exhibition inspired by the Demarco Archive to be presented at the European Parliament in Brussels. The first was entitled 'Beyond Conflict.' It was in response to the 9/11 tragedy, and forewords to the catalogue were contributed by HM Queen Elizabeth II and Nelson Mandela. The exhibition was focused on the cultural interface between the current histories of Europe as Christendom and the Islamic World.

The Signet Library provided the ideal environment for an exhibition inspired by the history of each and every Edinburgh Festival since the inaugural Edinburgh International Festival in 1947, contained within the Demarco Archive as a total artwork comprising event photographs, posters, diaries, programmes, prints, correspondence, drawings and paintings.

The exhibition ended with filmed conversation between myself and Amanda Catto as Visual Arts Director of Creative Scotland. This was introduced by Anna Bennett WS, Deputy Director of the Signet Library.

It was by her personal invitation that the exhibition took place.

The exhibition was filmed by Michael Lloyd and Marco Federici and was entitled 'Richard Demarco, 75 Years of the Edinburgh Festival.' It attracted sponsorship from *The Times* and *Sunday Times* newspapers and Burness Paull and Brewin Dolphin. It was accompanied by a programme which listed the highlights of the Edinburgh Festival and the Demarco Archives from 1947 to 2022. It was presented at the Signet Library to celebrate its 200th anniversary.

This exhibition brought back my memories of the dinner sponsored by George Riches, Director of the Phaidon Art Publishers. The three guest speakers were Lord Palumbo, Director of the Arts Council of England, Boris Biancheri, Italian Ambassador to the United Kingdom, and Sandy Nairne, Director of the National Portrait Gallery in London. Among the guests were Sir Sean and Lady Connery; Lady (Jean) Polwarth, Chairman of the Demarco Gallery; Leonard Friedman, founder of the Scottish Baroque Ensemble; Murray Grigor, former Director of the Edinburgh Film Festival and his late wife Barbara, Director of the Scottish Sculpture Trust.

I am truly indebted to Roddy Martine for taking the responsibility of writing the main text of *Demarco's Scotland* as his personal interpretation of what I have endeavoured to entwine as the history of Scotland with that of Continental Europe. I have had to endure several major challenges this year with regard to the safe-keeping of the Demarco Archive; these have occupied the precious time which I intended to dedicate to this publication. Roddy Martine's eloquence and his knowledge of Scotland's history has enabled this publication to come to fruition.

Richard Demarco, Edinburgh,
July 2024

I

Meikle Seggie Forever

JUST OVER ONE MILE FROM THE OFFICIAL SIGNPOST IN THE High STREET OF MILNATHORT YOU COULD COME ACROSS THIS LESS IMPRESSIVE SIGNPOST (NOT AT All AUTOMOBILE ASSOCIATION STANDARD) JUXTAPOSED WITH THE SIGN TO LEDLANET HOUSE, IN THE SEVENTIES, STILL THE HOME OF JOHN CALDER

IS MEIKLE SEGGIE JUST A FARM OR A LOST SETTLEMENT?

THE OCHIL HILLS ARE AN EXTENSION OF THE SIDLAW HILLS – THE WORLD OF MACBETH AND HIS CASTLE AT DUNSINANE AND OF GOWRIE. MACBETH'S THREE WITCHES?

THERE A MOMENT WHEN YOU CAN RESIST A MOZART OPERA AT LEDLANET AND THE LIFE ENHANCING WORLD CREATED BY JOHN CALDER IN THE OCHIL HILLS AND TURN TOWARDS MEIKLE SEGGIE?

What am I doing here?

SO, ONCE AND for all, what exactly is this Road to Meikle Seggie that so often features in the extraordinary life of Richard Demarco?

In his book *A Life in Pictures* (An Artwork Special from Northern Books 1995), Richard explains. The Road to Meikle Seggie does not lead to a town, village or hamlet but only to a farmyard of that name in Kinross on the Ledlanet estate of the late John Calder. It marks the site of an ancient settlement now considered too unimportant by map-makers to notice, and beyond that inconspicuous farmyard it leads to everything that exists in Scotland and beyond.

> The Road to Meikle Seggie should not be limited to this age. It does not fulfil the usual requirements of a modern road... It is a road at one with nature. It follows the lie of the land – rising, falling, turning and twisting, like a living thing. It does not detract in any way from the untouched landscape of rolling hills.
>
> The Road to Meikle Seggie is the gateway to the Scotland that eludes most Sassenachs (and surely that includes most tourists). It will take you through the valley between the Cleish and Lomond Hills where you will first glimpse the Ochil Hills as the introduction to the wild, unspoiled, unchanging mountainous land where the elemental forces are forever in control.

The great abbeys, country houses and landed estates of Scotland with their tenanted farms, crofting communities and traditions are all part of The Road to Meikle Seggie – a lost village where once 200 people lived on the great publisher John Calder's Ledlanet family estate, gainfully employed in the Calder brewery producing Calder Ale. It was therefore considered important in the world of the Demarco Gallery for it to become Scotland's equivalent of Black Mountain College which was essentially a cattle ranch in the Black Mountains of North Carolina, the American version of The Bauhaus.

The Meikle Seggie that once featured on a Kinross signpost is of equal symbolic importance to that of Stirling, Cupar and St Andrews. Alongside the lost villages of Scotland is the lost history of their inhabitants, many of whom are our ancestors.

Scotland is therefore NOT all about the tourist destinations of Edinburgh, Glasgow, the Trossachs, Aberdeen, Inverness and the Highlands and Islands. It is so much bigger than that. This book is the profound expression of the deeply held and timeless love affair of two passionate European Scots for a so often misunderstood global Caledonian utopia.

It is a celebration of what the Scots-born composer Hamish MacCunn called *The Land of the Mountain and the Flood*, its impact upon the world and the opportunities it has over the centuries provided for artistic endeavour throughout the world. 'What am I doing here?' is the everlasting *cri de coeur*, alongside 'How lucky am I to be here!'

Journeys and explorations

All of our lives involve journeys of one sort or another; a voyage through time, emotion and landscape. A voyage of discovery. A voyage of introspection. A voyage of failure. A voyage of achievement.

We are all explorers. For the lucky ones, there is nowhere else in this universe where such a diversity of riches and folklore is so readily embraced than on the roadsides and hinterland of Scotland, signposted without prejudice for all to discover.

On The Road to Meikle Seggie are a series of landmarks leading from the mists of an all too evasive continental pre-history into the remnants of a glorious, often violent inheritance, onwards towards an uncertain future where Scotland's creative brilliance, past and present, are the only certainties.

Everything is made possible on The Road to Meikle Seggie. It leads not only from the Edinburgh Festivals of the 1960s and 1970s. It leads to the farmscapes of Mellerstain House, Johnny Watson's East Lothian Skateraw Farm and to certain 'gardenscapes', in particular, Ian Hamilton Finlay's Stonypath Farm in Lanarkshire and the farmscapes of Dumfries and Galloway painted by Archie Sutter Watt, as well as the botanic gardens of Edinburgh and Benmore. It leads to the Border abbeys of Melrose, Dryburgh, Kelso, Pluscarden and Nunraw; to the prehistoric sites of Callanish, the Ring of Brodgar, Maeshowe, Cairnpapple, Kilmartin Valley; the estates and libraries of Falkland

Palace, Traquair House; the houses and studios of Margot Sandeman on the Isle of Arran, Edna Whyte on the island of Luing; the farmscape of Dalmeny House; the Roman sites at Trimontium, Cramond, the Antonine Wall at Falkirk; the farmscapes abutting the Crinan Canal and the houses and estates of Marion Campbell of Kilberry in Knapdale and on the Isle of Harris where, in her early teens, she constructed her own loom to weave outstanding examples of Harris Tweed well into her 80s.

The point of writing all of this down is that there are countless alternative sources of material to be studied and utilised within the histories of those given the task of 'stewardship'; that is the caring for historic places identified within the history of Scotland from prehistoric times to the present day.

And to underline how the history of the Edinburgh Festival must be re-rooted in that of the whole of Scotland is because the Edinburgh Festival was a direct response to the global sufferings of Europe caused by the Second World War.

How many of us are aware that the second language of Scotland is Polish? If you study the physical fabric of the interiors of Dalkeith Palace or Falkland Palace, or Menzies Castle in Perthshire, or Black Barony Castle near Peebles, you will find evidence that the Polish Army left behind an indelible mark.

Forty thousand Scots found gainful employment as long ago as the 15th century in Poland, and many Polish place and family names have their origins in the language of the Scots. The Demarco Gallery, founded in the 1960s, was totally reliant upon artists from that country to reveal how the cultural integrity of Scotland is deeply wedded into that of Poland, and to its adjoining countries such as Belarus, Lithuania and Moldova.

At the same time, The Road to Meikle Seggie, which most probably had its origins as a drovers' road, is also a pilgrimage road, connecting the Isle of Iona and the Orcadian cathedral of St Magnus and the Outer Hebridean medieval church dedicated to St Clemens. For over a thousand years it has never been possible to separate those drovers' roads and the Celtic pilgrimage routes from the coastlines of Dumfries and Galloway and Kintyre, and County Down and County Antrim in Ireland.

Within the pages of this book are to be found the nodal points that inspired the EDINBURGH ARTS programmes from the 1970s onwards in close collaboration with Edinburgh University's School of Scottish Studies, under the direction of Professor John MacQueen, as well as the School of Extra-Mural Studies piloted by Dr Basil Skinner, co-founder of the Hopetoun Trust.

It is so important for the reader to understand that the history of the British Empire we once knew and admired so much is irredeemably European. For example, why was it that on his visits to Scotland, the great avant-garde German artist Joseph Beuys was so determined to visit the graves of Adam Smith in Edinburgh and Sir Walter Scott in Dryburgh Abbey, buried alongside Field Marshal The Earl Haig?

Through EDINBURGH ARTS, great adventures were embarked upon and great international friendships forged, thus cementing the cultural and artistic triumphs of Scotland and leading to the Demarco Gallery's remarkable engagement with Scandinavia, Poland, Russia, the Balkans, Austria, France and notably with the Venice Biennale in Italy.

'It was impossible to grow up, as I did, in Edinburgh, without being aware of Richard Demarco,' reflects the broadcaster and journalist Sheena McDonald, a former Chair of The Traverse Theatre.

'Long before I met him, I knew of his pioneering work as an arts entrepreneur. He was then based in Melville Crescent, and his reach extended throughout the city. A child of Italian immigrants, his perspective was unfailingly internationalist, and his contribution to Edinburgh culture, during the festive summer months in particular, cemented the city's reputation as a centre of artistic excellence.

'My formative years were continuously enriched by his projects and introductions. I was at university in 1976 when I saw Tadeusz Kantor's mesmerising *Dead Class* at Edinburgh College of Art, universally admired around the world for its theatrical exploration of history, cannot be undone, influential beyond compass but never matched. Thank you, Ricky – and thank you for bringing Theatre Obala from Sarajevo to the the Edinburgh Festival with *The Yellow Rabbit* and *Tattoo Theatre*. The power of European theatre illuminated festive Edinburgh thanks to Richard Demarco.'

Sheena was also impressed with the reactions of the citizens of the capital of Bosnia and their local media to new ideas and artworks – and also by the pervasive enthusiasm (which she didn't share) for cigarette smoking!

'Ricky took my hand and ran me through the streets of Sarajevo to a corner where the impression of footprints was petrified in the pavement,' she recalled.

This was where Gavrilo Princip was standing in June 1914 when Archduke Franz Ferdinand's open car drove by, he told her, excitedly. History was made here – the world would never be the same again.

'Of course Sarajevo is not the same today,' Sheena said. 'The footprints along with so much else were obliterated during the killing years of the 1990s when the city was besieged by Bosnian Serbs during their genocide campaign through the former Yugoslavia against Bosnian Muslims. I visited the city a couple of times during the siege and was able to interview artists living through the carnage. I smuggled out some small prints which represented a much larger exhibition, *Witnesses of Existence*, which had been invited to tour the world, including the Venice Biennale, but which had been denied access by the Serbs.

'My precious smuggled booty was framed and exhibited by Richard Demarco at the 1994 Edinburgh Festival Fringe. And the producer of *Yellow Rabbit* has become a friend too, captaining the Sarajevo Film Festival from 1995 (when the city was besieged) for over 20 years.'

Jonathan Gibbs, former Programme Director of Illustration at Edinburgh College of Art School of Design, vividly remembers their first encounter. A phone call came out of the blue: 'Is this Jonathan Gibbs?' It was a young American woman in Edinburgh.

In 1979 I had sent off my slides and cv and Richard Demarco liked my work. Was I free to exhibit in a month's time?

I drove with a van-load of work from my family home in Suffolk to Scotland. This was a solo exhibition; 20 or so framed pieces to be carried up the stairs of Monteith House, 61 High Street. Whilst hanging them, Kenneth Rowntree came into the gallery and talked to me about my work. This was deeply impressive, a Professor from Newcastle, no less!

Ricky also was deeply impressive and compelling. At that early stage of my career there had been few sales or reviews both of which came from this event. I am eternally grateful.

Whenever we have met over the intervening 45 years, he remembers my work at that time and asks what I am

25

making now. 'Now!' Ricky communicates great vitality, encouragement and impetus. From that first encounter, he has been an unforgettable, inspirational and extraordinary figure.

Finding himself shunned by the politics of the Scottish arts establishment during the 1980s, Richard Demarco stoically realised he would have to plough his own furrow and he has done so ever since. As he is the first to acknowledge, he was by that stage of his career blessed with a raft of friends and admirers who were not only willing to help but in a position to lend their support.

By courting these Renaissance patrons, Richard Demarco was able to expand the Edinburgh Festival into some of the most spectacular corners of Scotland, and beyond into continental Europe, notably Italy, Poland, the Balkans and Scandinavia where the name Demarco is revered to this day.

Terry Ann Newman perfectly captures the thrilling, unbounded nature of Demarco's vision:

'The Road to Meikle Seggie is an itinerant university, constantly in flux and accumulating students of every kind, be they young, old, infirm or uneducated. For me, this is the main art work and achievement of the life of Richard Demarco. He is naturally and constantly a teacher. He embraces not only the mind but also the soul. In fact, it is really the soul that he sees, embraces and leads onwards. One of his favourite saints is St Bernadette. She was a simple girl, made to clean floors and stairs and belittled by her fellow contemplatives.

'However, Richard is of a most serious intellect, enabling diverse conversations with anyone. His sense of connecting thoughts, ideas and situations is enviable.

Richard ranges through history and mythology, intertwines them and arrives at the truth, the truth that is to be found in the mystical world of fairy tales.'

2

But first you have to know your European history

28/5 19/98

THE CROATIA – SCOTLAND CULTURAL DIALOGUE

TYPICAL GIRL'S COSTUME GIVING VISUAL EVIDENCE OF A FOLKLORE MAINTAINED OVER MANY GENERATIONS BY THE VILLAGE OF PREKOPAKRA

PREKOPAKRA SELO OD DAVNINA FOLKSONG COMPANY SINGING IN CROATIAN LANGUAGE FROM THE CROATIAN VILLAGE OF PREKOPAKRA

THE NATIONAL CROATIAN COLOURS OF RED, WHITE AND BLUE ARE PREDOMINANT.

CROATIAN LANGUAGE

NINUŠKA SE DJEVOJČICA POSKO ČILA

NINUŠKA SE DJEVOJCICA NA VRBOVOJ GRANIČICI KRAJ NJE PALA TANKA STAZA STAZOM IDE MLADO MOMČE. " ID' OTHLE DJEVOJCICE TA JE VRBA KRHKO DRVO SAVIN ČE SE, PREKIN ČE SE, TI SI MLADA, UBI' ČEŠ SE ! "

THE TEXT OF THE MANY OLD FOLK SONGS COLLECTED OVER THE PAST 50 YEARS BY ANDRIJA ŠIRAC WERE SUNG BY AN ENSEMBLE OF DANCERS AND SINGERS ESTABLISHED IN 1929. THEY ARE KNOWN AS KUD-A SELJACKA SIDRALE

THEY CHERISH THE TRADITION OF TAMBURA PLAYING. THE SONGS ARE MOST OFTEN INTERPRETED BY A SINGING GROUP WITHOUT INSTRUMENTAL ACCOMPANIMENT WHEN A SOLO SINGER HAS A KEY ROLE BOTH IN SONG AND DANCE — " POSKOCIZA AND KORAČNICA "

THEY WERE WELCOMED IN DUNDEE BY THE PROVOST — MERVYN ROLFE — THEY LATER PERFORMED AT THE McMANUS CIVIC GALLERY IN DUNDEE AT A CIVIC RECEPTION AND LATER AT LORD ALEXANDER DUNDEE'S HOUSE AT BIRKHILL — HE IS THE HONORARY CROATIAN CONSUL IN SCOTLAND

THE CROATIAN FOLKSONG COMPANY PERFORMED IN THE DEBATING CHAMBER OF THE ROYAL HIGH SCHOOL

THIS GROUP OF CROATIAN FOLK SINGERS PERFORMED IN THE RICHARD DEMARCO FOUNDATION 1998 EDINBURGH FRINGE FESTIVAL PROGRAMME IN NEW PARLIAMENT HOUSE

THIS PROGRAMME CELEBRATED A CULTURAL DIALOGUE BETWEEN CROATIA AND SCOTLAND — BETWEEN THE EDINBURGH AND DUBROVNIK, FESTIVALS

Scotland and Europe

IN THE YEAR 1435 the Italian-born Aeneas Sylvius Piccolomini, the future Pope Pius II, was despatched upon a secret mission to Scotland by Cardinal Albergati, Pope Eugene IV's legate. From an impoverished noble background, the 34-year-old Piccolomini recognised a great career opportunity when he saw it.

As it turned out, the winter voyage was anything but plain sailing. When the prelate's ship was caught in a violent storm off the Haddingtonshire coast, he was forced to disembark at Dunbar. To give thanks for his survival, he fell to his knees and vowed to walk barefoot to the nearest shrine dedicated to Our Lady.

One wonders if anyone actually explained to him that this would involve a ten-mile hike over frozen fields to the village of Whitekirk. He was to suffer from rheumatism for the remainder of his days.

Piccolomini's specific mission, in the age of foot travel, horseback and boat transport, was to consolidate the diplomatic relationship that existed between Rome and James I, King of Scots. However, the underlying reason as to why this might have been necessary at the time remains a mystery.

A belated amends for the Vatican having excommunicated King James' great-great-grandfather Robert the Bruce a century earlier? Unlikely.

Or was it simply to ruffle an ongoing and uneasy friction between Scotland and Henry VI of England?

Speculation aside, what Piccolomini's visit underlined was the high regard in which the medieval kingdom of Scots, regardless of political posturing, was held by the Papal States, further emphasised by the Papal gifts of an Italian-made silver gilt sceptre from Pope Alexander VI to James IV in 1494, and the Sword of State from Pope Julius II to James IV in 1507. Both of these treasures are today housed in the splendid Crown Room of Edinburgh Castle and recognised as integral parts of the Honours of Scotland.

What they serve to confirm in all of their shining splendour is that this small nation of Scotland has occupied a recognisable slot at the very heart of European civilisation for over a thousand years. In 1072, when King Malcolm III and his Hungarian-born Saxon wife Saint Margaret faced off against the army of William the Conqueror at Abernethy, the invader William recognised the Norse threads of the lineage they had in common and uncharacteristically backed off. In the years that followed, Malcolm's son, Alexander I of Scotland, was betrothed to William's illegitimate daughter

Sybilla of Normandy, and the future Henry I of England married King Malcolm and Queen Margaret's daughter Princess Matilda of Scotland (Good Queen Maud), thus for the first time introducing the bloodline of the Royal House of Dunkeld into the Anglo-Norman ascendancy across continental Europe.

In 1320, when the barons of Scotland petitioned yet another Pope (John XXII) from Arbroath Abbey to remove his excommunication order over Robert the Bruce, they were simply asserting their status as oligarchs belonging to a European nation.

When Edward I of England first marched into Scotland in 1296 and carried off most of the Scottish Royal Archive, it was intentional genocide. To neuter your enemies, you need to have control of, and preferably obliterate, their records. Oliver Cromwell was to act in a similar manner in 1650.

But the full tragedy befell ten years later when a merchant vessel, *Elizabeth of Burntisland*, returning a cargo of 86 hogshead barrels containing two tons of paperwork relating to the entire Scots Archive, sank off the Northumbrian coast, thus plunging Scotland's history into the Dark Ages.

Hidden Charters and documents have since emerged to fill some of the gaps, but it is nonetheless a struggle to unearth what truly went on pre-14th century. As a multi-cultural race, however, the Scots were far too canny not to understand the sweeping importance of their recorded heritage, a fact symbolised by the Lia Fáil, the inaugural Stone of Destiny, from which all of Scotland's previous rulers were proclaimed, and which has its origins in far off Palestine. We may never know if that which is displayed in the Perth Museum is the real thing or as chronicled by the novelist Nigel Tranter in his 1991 novel *The Stone*, a magnificent practical hoax perpetrated by the Abbot of Scone.

Edward Longshanks, never a man to miss a trick, fully comprehended the significance of this biblical artefact which no doubt explains the credibility surrounding the lump of unimpressive sandstone hauled off to Westminster only to be returned 600 years later.

In his foreword to *Scottish Clan & Family Names, Their Arms, Origins & Tartans,* first published in 1987, Sir Malcolm Innes of Edingight KCVO, that most munificent of Lord Lyon King of Arms, observed:

> Those of us who are familiar with the emigration from Scotland
> from the Depression of the 1930s, the post-war difficulties and

the high unemployment that persisted in Scotland, perhaps find it difficult to appreciate that for 200 years between 1097 and 1296, the high road to Scotland was an attractive prospect for the younger sons of English families and those of continental origin. At the close of the eleventh century, Scotland held a mixture of Celtic and pre-Celtic peoples: the Picts, the Britons, the Irish (Scots), and also the Anglo-Saxons and Scandinavians.

Somehow it is hard to imagine that in the 12th century the population of Scotland, sparsely distributed throughout mainland and islands, was estimated to have been in the region of 50,000.

It was therefore a clever ruse of monarchs of old, David I, his predecessors, his brothers and his successors, to control their realm through the scattered strategic monasteries of the Catholic faith: the Dominicans, Cistercians and Tironensians from France; the Benedictines, Trinitarians and Franciscans from Italy; the Carmelites originating in Israel, and the Culdees from Ireland. Such fundamental establishments served as a communication network between religious houses the length and breadth of the British Isles and beyond into continental Europe and Scandinavia.

Contrary to the contemporary image, there was nothing insular or reclusive about these religious retreats. The monasteries and nunneries of Europe knew exactly what was going on in the wider world, especially when their occupants, at least some of them, indulged in vows of silence. More importantly, they kept records of the past, a prime example being the *Scotichronicon,* compiled in the 15th century by Walter Bower, Canon Regular of Inchcolm Abbey, a continuation of *Chronica Gentis Scotorum,* the work of John of Fordun, a secular priest in the previous century.

It was the Calvinist Kirk and Reformation of the 16th century that finally put a stop to their purpose, albeit those of a more cynical nature might find some amusement in discovering just how many priests of the old order in Scotland transitioned into Kirk of Scotland ministers overnight.

What this goes on to show is that medieval Scotland, a largely impoverished rural and coastal society before the Age of Enlightenment and Industrial Revolution sprinkled their magic dust, was never parochial in promoting a world outlook.

As early as the 12th century, David I encouraged Flemish settlers to import their entrepreneurial skills and returned the compliment on mainland Belgium. The export of wool, weaving, herring, salmon, cod and wheat from Aberdeen, Dundee, Leith and Berwick to Zeeland and Holland, was also early on encouraged by the marriage of James II of Scotland to Mary of Guelders, grand-niece of Philip the Good, Duke of Burgundy and his wife Isabella of Portugal.

Little boats with their passengers and cargo commuted back and forth day and night. Trade prospered on all sides. To this day there exists a museum in the form of a Scottish House in the old staple port of Veere. In the later 18th and 19th centuries, shipbuilding and sailings from the seaports of Clyde, Aberdeen, Dundee and Leith dominated the sea routes of the world. Mid-millennium, Scots mercenaries joined the armies of continental Europe, the armies of Christian IV of Denmark and Gustavus Adolphus of Sweden.

Étienne Macdonald, son of an exiled Jacobite army veteran rose through the ranks of the French army to become a Marshal of the French Empire and a military leader during the French Revolutionary and Napoleonic Wars. Patrick Gordon from Auchleuchries became a general in the Russian Army and forged a close friend of Tsar Peter the Great. Similarly, Count Yakov Alexandrovich Bruce also served as a general in the Russian Army. The Scottish Royalist general Tam Dalyell of The Binns saw Russian service under the sobriquet of the Muscovite Devil.

Prince Michael Barclay de Tolly from the Towie, Aberdeenshire family became a Field Marshal and Russia's Minister of War during Napoleon's 1820 invasion. Mikhail Lermontov, a descendant of the 13th-century Scottish poet Thomas the Rhymer, also known as Thomas Learmonth from Earlston in the Scottish Borders, died in battle in the Smolensk War.

Peter the Great visited the dockyards of Leith incognito to study shipbuilding, and Catherine the Great co-opted the Edinburgh architect Charles Cameron to dramatically reinvent St Petersburg. By the 1600s there were an estimated 30,000 Scots living in Poland and the Dyce-born Alexander Chalmers was four times Mayor of the city of Warsaw.

It is mostly forgotten that Charles Philippe, Comte d'Artois, younger brother of the executed Louis XVI of France was permitted by the British Government to take up residence at Holyrood (designated a sanctuary) in 1796, following his escape from Paris. When he arrived, the citizens of Edinburgh, despite a few republican rumblings, turned out en masse to welcome him, and he stayed at Holyrood for seven years before returning to France to be crowned Charles X.

However, following the second French Revolution, he was back in

Scotland with his grandson Henri Duke of Bordeaux who had briefly occupied the French throne as the last Bourbon king. Meanwhile, Henri's father, the Duke of Angoulême, his mother Marie Thérèse, daughter of Louis XVI and Queen Marie Antoinette, therefore Charles's niece, and their sister-in-law Caroline de Bourbon-Sicily, Duchess de Berry, made their home in Regent Terrace overlooking Holyrood Park.

Ironically, it was an American, Arthur L Herman who in 2001 first wrote the book entitled *How the Scots Created the Modern World: The True Story of How Western Europe's Poorest Country Created Our World And Everything In It*, a theme subsequently picked up and embellished by the home-based historian Sir Tom Devine.

A vast number of Scots colonised North America and Canada, notably Nova Scotia, and Australia. The Glasgow-born Sir John Macdonald was the first Prime Minister of Canada; the Isle of Mull-born Lachlan Macquarie was the fifth Governor of New South Wales; for better or worse, 34 Presidents of the United States of America have claimed Scottish descent.

Scotland's greatest gift to the world has been itself, its culture, its creativity, the extraordinary ability of its people to integrate and celebrate what truly matters in global terms, friendship and decency. Add in our greatest export, Scotch Whisky; our iconic clan and family tartans; our golf courses and musical traditions, and you have an identity that is instantly recognisable and internationally respected and loved. Wear a kilt in Manhattan or Montmartre and you make friends for life.

Such achievements were in no way achieved through inward introspection. This is not about narrow nationalism. Scotland as an integral part of the United Kingdom of Great Britain remains uniquely European. Hence Richard Demarco's Road to Meikle Seggie is the ultimate destination and catalyst for the global history of ideas.

And that in so many ways explains the Scots' genius for invention – Kirkpatrick Macmillan and the bicycle; James Watt and the steam engine; Alexander Graham Bell and the telephone, John Loudon McAdam and tarmac and asphalt concrete; Sir James Young Simpson and chloroform; Sir Alexander Fleming and penicillin; the Edinburgh domiciled Peter Higgs and the Higgs boson particle.

So many of our ancestors were in on the adventure from the start and shared and, in their own ways, prospered as a result. The Road to Meikle Seggie unashamedly embraces them all. Scotland is so much bigger than the Edinburgh Festival. It is all-embracing.

For those who ignore our history, and such a history it is, the voices of the past shall inevitably come back to haunt them.

Divine intervention

The ruins of Holyrood Abbey with its adjoining royal palace set within extensive parkland under the looming bulk of Arthur's Seat, Edinburgh's crouching lioness, was inspirational to Richard Demarco from his childhood and it was therefore only to be expected that it would be featured in the EDINBURGH ARTS expedition of 1972. The excursion began in the ruined abbey and progressed to climbing the Radical Road on Salisbury Crags to study the site of James Hutton's 18th-century analysis of the Basaltic Rock, wallowing in fiction of James Hogg's *Confessions of a Justified Sinner*, and to inspect the charming hillside folly of St Anthony's Chapel and holy wells above St Margaret's Loch.

So much of Scotland's golden age is etched into the reality of Holyrood Park: the crouching bulk of Arthur's Seat, its name derived from ancient Strathclyde; Salisbury Crags, known long ago as the Crags of the Dead; the Radical Road built with the sweat of reactionary west of Scotland weavers and the romantic ruined folly of St Anthony's Chapel, the exact origins of which are intriguingly unknown. It was only to be expected that it be embraced by the creative energy of those who took part in that pioneering EDINBURGH ARTS adventure of 1972.

The Road to Meikle Seggie therefore begins in Holyrood Park. The story goes that in the autumn of 1127, while deer hunting in the Royal Forest of Drumsheugh below Arthur's Seat to the east of Edinburgh, the 43-year-old King David I of Scotland was thrown from his horse when it was startled by a stag.

On tumbling to the ground, he was confronted by 'a muckle white hart (stag)', whereupon the vision of a glowing crucifix miraculously appeared between the stag's antlers and the beast backed off.

King David's mother, the beatified Queen Margaret, had been gifted a fragment of the biblical True Cross from Waltham Abbey in England and had brought it to Scotland on her marriage to Malcolm III. In profound gratitude for his escape from death, King David vowed to build a great abbey on the site below Salisbury Crags and to dedicate it to the 'Holy Rude'.

David had already instructed for the Benedictine Abbey of the Holy

Trinity and Saint Margaret to be built at Dunfermline and the Tironensian House at Kelso. He went on to create religious houses at Melrose in 1136, Jedburgh around 1138 and Dryburgh in 1150. In those days, Scottish monarchs consistently moved around their realm, occupying accommodation provided by the church. At Holyrood, a mile from the stronghold of Edinburgh Castle, Stewart kings and queens lodged at the guest house situated to the west of the abbey cloister. The Augustinian monastic house he founded at Holyrood became the template for the principal residence of the Royal House of Scotland.

As has been revealed from 20th-century excavations, the completed building of the 12th and early 13th centuries comprised a six-bay aisled choir, three-bay transepts with a central tower above and an eight-bay aisled nave with twin towers at its western front. Established around the abbey was a five-mile area of sanctuary comprising most of modern day Holyrood Park. Here, felons and debtors could appeal for protection and if pardoned might have been given lodgings in the buildings that surrounded the abbey.

With its ups and down, it was a golden age for Scotland. The nobility and Prelates of Scotland met at Holyrood to discuss raising a ransom for William the Lion, held prisoner by his cousin Henry II of England since the Battle of Alnwick in 1174. Five years later, the Papal legate Cardinal Vivian, carrying a commission from Pope Alexander III, held a Council at the abbey church to cement Hibernian–Scottish Papal relations.

Between 1256 and 1410, Scotland's parliament was convened here eight times notably in 1328 by Robert the Bruce to sign the Treaty of Edinburgh–Northampton which concluded the First War of Scottish Independence.

Over the following two centuries, however, the abbey church of Holyrood came regularly under attack from invading English armies. Notwithstanding this, it was between 1488 and 1501 that James IV began work on a royal palace essentially to impress his incoming bride Princess Margaret Tudor. The abbey refectory was converted into a Great Hall and certainly by 1507 it has become a palace of merriment with regular dances, banquets and tournaments.

Alas, the destruction of the abbey began with the Rough Wooing when the invading English armies under the Earl of Hertford inflicted considerable damage mid-16th century, and then two decades later the Scottish Reformation wrought its havoc when a mob destroyed the altars and looted its treasures. In 1569, Adam Bothwell, Commendator of

Holyrood, advised the General Assembly of the Church of Scotland that the east end of the church was in such a state that the choir and transept required to be demolished. In 1633, the abbey was extensively remodelled for the Coronation of Charles 1 undertaken with full Anglican rites, but by 1688, the remaining Protestant congregation had moved to worship in the nearby Kirk of the Canongate. Extensive renovation did take place but in 1766 the abbey was closed on safety grounds. In 1768, the roof collapsed. Such is mortality.

3

All in the mind's eye

MAGNUS MAGNUSSON AS A SCOTSMAN JOURNALIST AND BILL WATSON, THE EDITOR OF SCOTSMAN ON SUNDAY AND HIS WIFE CATHERINE ROBINS REGARD 29 FREDERICK ST. AS A SALON

IT WAS IN 29 FREDERICK STREET THAT SANDY NAIRNE AND SALLY HOLMAN BROUGHT TADEUSZ KANTOR TO BE INTRODUCED TO JOSEPH BEUYS THIS RESULTED IN JOSEPH BEUYS PARTICIPATING IN TADEUSZ KANTOR'S CRICOT THEATRE PRODUCTION OF "LOVELIES AND DOWDIES" AT THE RICHARD DEMARCO GALLERYS PLAY ENTITLED "LOVELIES AND DOWDIES" AT THE RICHARD DEMARCO EDINBURGH FESTIVAL FORREST HILL POORHOUSE — FOR THE 1973 OFFICIAL EDINBURGH FESTIVAL AND TERRI LANE'S ALSO — THE TRAVERSE ACTORS: CLIVE POLIT, ROSANNO DICKSON THE TRAVERSE DIRECTOR

TO JOSEPH BEUYS AND TADEUSZ KANTOR TO EACH OTHER

IT WAS IN 1983 THAT RICHARD & LAINE DEMARCO INVITED MR & MRS. COLIN THOMSON AND IL CONTESSA PANZA DI BIUMO TO HAVE DINNER AT 29 FREDERICK STREET AND IL CONTESSA PANZA DI BIUMO TO DISCUSS THE POSSIBILITY OF HAVING THE PANZA ART COLLECTION IN SCOTLAND TO DISCUSS THE PANZA PREMIER SHEILA COLVIN ALL MET AT No 29!

VIEW OF EDINBURGH CASTLE FROM KITCHEN WINDOW OF 29 FREDERICK STREET. — A TOP FLOOR 18TH CENTURY FLAT IN THE CENTRE OF EDINBURGH'S NEW TOWN IT WAS IN THIS NEW TOWN FLAT THAT TOM MITCHELL, THE PATRON OF THE TRAVERSE MET JOHN MARTIN ANDREW ELLIOTT AN JAMES WALKER THE 3 PATRONS OF THE TRAVERSE

IT WAS HERE THAT THE FOUNDERS OF THE TRAVERSE THEATRE CLUB & ARTS GALLERY MET FROM 1957 TO 1963 PLANNING TO ESTABLISH THE TRAVERSE AS AN ENLARGEMENT OF THE PAPERBACK BOOKSHOP AMONG EDINBURGH FESTIVAL VISITORS TO THIS FLAT WERE ROY DOTRICE PETER MCENERY AND DAVID BUCK JOHNNY DANKWORTH AND CLEO LANE AND YVGENY YEVTUSHENKO

GAIL PENDER, PETE MCGINN, TOM MACPHAIL, MIKE MCLAUGHLIN, FRAN & JINNIE MACPHAIL

A stunning visual record

THERE IS AN often overlooked element of Richard Demarco's remarkable multi-faceted creative existence and that is his formidable talent as an artist. For almost a century, he has produced literally thousands of drawings, sketches and paintings emanating from his early life classes at Edinburgh College of Art, where a young Sean Connery was among his models, to detailed works in pen, ink and watercolour of the landscapes and vernacular buildings that have caught his eye. The visual record he leaves behind him is breathtaking. Yet it is for his teaching skills, his ability to inspire, his cultural promotion of others and formidable energy, that he is perhaps better known.

From 1949 to 1953, he studied book illustration, typography, printmaking and mural painting at Edinburgh College of Art. As Secretary of the Edinburgh College of Art Sketch Club, he gained his first experience in organising exhibitions, and first showed his own drawings and water colours at the Society of Scottish Artists in 1961, followed in 1962 by his first one-man exhibition at the Douglas & Foulis Gallery in Edinburgh's Castle Street.

Those early mixed-media exhibitions were immensely well received and paved the way for the future, but it was a future largely dedicated to displaying the works of others. Spurred on by art critics of the calibre of first of all Edward 'Teddy' Gage, then especially the legendary Cordelia Oliver, all three represented a generation of intense perceptive talent, unafraid of grasping the shock of the new.

Artist and storyteller Lizzie McDougall has known Richard since she was ten years old as he and Jim Haynes were frequent visitors to her parents' house. 'My father helped them set up the Traverse Theatre, and then Daddy was Ricky's chairman trying to keep the Scottish Arts Council from stopping him!' she recalled.

'My house is full of his paintings that he has given to either my parents or my children and I love and appreciate them because as well as the extraordinary things he has done for the arts and people, I think he is a very fine artist.

'He has been a huge influence on my life, the inspiration for my commitment to bringing the arts to as many people as possible in the Highlands through producing and promoting arts activities, although my efforts are tiny in comparison to Ricky's amazing achievements, he is a blessing to this world and I love him dearly.'

Said painter and arts historian Andrew Brown, founder of the 369 Gallery: 'I was berated for a quote attributed to me in the press in the 1980s when I said that Richard Demarco was John the Baptist to my Jesus Christ. Forgive my blasphemy but I meant that like John the Baptist he was 'the one who came before' and that when I graduated from Edinburgh College of Art in 1977, Demarco was the only independent 'galleriest' in Scotland who had an international outlook and reputation. I followed in his footsteps and set up the 369 Gallery in 1978 to promote young Scottish artists abroad but even now almost half a century later in his mid-90's, he is still forging ahead and I'm left in his wake!'

Richard's friend Arthur Watson, Senior Lecturer at Duncan of Jordanstone College of Art & Design, and former President of the Royal Scottish Academy, observed in his 2020 tribute to Richard Demarco, 'He continues to respond to his surroundings through the making of lyrical watercolour drawings in direct line from the English artist-illustrators who inspired him as a student. But even this seemingly traditional approach can be re-cast as an endless visual journey on his quest for spiritual enlightenment "on The Road to Meikle Seggie" through Scotland to Eastern Europe and the Mediterranean.'

Others wholeheartedly agree.

'Richard Demarco has demonstrated for me convincingly that art in its many forms cannot be suppressed, and is far greater than a genteel entertainment,' insists Sheena McDonald. 'And he is himself an artist. I am proud to own three or four artworks by him – a print of the creels in St Monan's Harbour in Fife; a small townscape of James Court at the top of the Royal Mile, the first home of the Traverse Theatre (of which, of course, Ricky was one of the pioneering 'midwives'!) and a Meikle Seggie landscape, illustrating his enduring passion for Scotland.

'He has, over the years, staged brief exhibitions of his own work. There is always time for another, I think. His mastery of yet more media is complementary to his skill as a promoter of others' work. His own work surely merits greater respect and acclaim.'

The painter Hugh Buchanan, whose works are in the collections of King Charles III and the late Queen Mother, concurs with this and has long been an admirer. 'When my parents moved into their first army quarters in the early 1960s, my maternal grandmother, Molly Ross, an artist herself, asked my father what sort of pictures they were going to put on the walls,' he recalls.

'My father had no idea and only owned two pictures – prints. One was of a Black Watch soldier in a kilt and bearskin, the other of the Siege of Sevastopol. My grandmother was obviously unimpressed by this meagre and very conventional collection, so she suggested he visit two exhibitions that were on at that time in Edinburgh.

'One featured the paintings of a young woman called Joan Eardley; the other by a young man called Demarco. My father came back with three Joan Eardleys and a lovely watercolour by Ricky of Wireworks Close.

'"Will this do?" he asked my grandmother. Apparently it did. My mother still cherishes those pictures.'

Clare Henry, British art critic, columnist, curator and print maker has been a friend and Demarco supporter since she was Chief Art Critic of the *Glasgow Herald*.

'Forty-five years ago I reviewed an exhibition at Glasgow's top venue, The Third Eye Centre, in Sauchiehall Street, with the eye-catching title of "Demarco's Road to Meikle Seggie".

'I knew Demarco as a charismatic impresario, but not his work. Greeted by an array of architectural pen drawings and watercolours from Edinburgh to Italy, I quickly realised I was looking at the work of a skilled professional with a gift for capturing topography in lively line and assured easy gesture.

'The show's theme, "The Road" as a symbol of our journey through life, is a favourite Demarco preoccupation. And in 1978, I enjoyed distant views or glimpses through rock cleft, the more to entice exploration. Paired drawings: a doorway to the Orkney Isles' Iron Age Midhowe Broch entrance next to Malta's Temple of Mnajdra, provided international excitement.

'Back then my only disappointment was the realistic, mundane stretch of road to his iconic Meikle Seggie, drawn not as the entry to a magic land, but something ordinary, everyday. The works were for sale, several cityscapes already snapped up.

'The public love Demarco's work, as numerous fundraisers can testify. But curatorial admiration is a different thing. I went on to see and sometimes review many more shows of Demarco's work, thousands of drawings.

'Demarco, the charismatic celebrity, exotic entrepreneur, brilliant teacher, speaker, mentor to many, is an inveterate artist, a pen or pencil always in his hand – but sadly under-appreciated as an artist.

'Why? Well, he never had a studio, didn't paint big oils; nor did he chase dealers or curators for himself. In fact, he rarely talked about his own work being far too busy promoting the radical work of others. As time went on Ricky's natural talent as a draughtsman was taken for granted, his colourful landscapes too.

'In 1983 I also regrettably followed the trend. My review of his Edinburgh Torrance Gallery show mentions drawings "done at speed – often while conducting an interview," and adds that his works were "Surprisingly conventional compared to his avant-garde enthusiasms."

'There you have it! Demarco's work was not taken seriously because everyone expected radical, cutting-edge work. They forget that he's a romantic who loves his subject matter, loves every stone of picturesque Edinburgh, adores his Italian homeland. His aim is sympathetic realisation not outrageous interpretation. He saves his immense talents for galvanising a lifetime of memorable arts events of every kind.

'And thereby hangs another story. The Venice Biennale 1990!

'Like many others I have hundreds of Demarco anecdotes but the best dates from spring 1988. I happened to mention I was taking my 12-year-old daughter to Venice at half-term. Quick as a flash Ricky waved his arms and exclaimed, "While you're there, find me a venue for Scottish artists to celebrate Glasgow City of Culture – anywhere in the city, maybe a deconsecrated church, an old hotel, or a decrepit palazzo!"

'He threw the baton. I picked it up. With great good fortune, luck was on my side. Having met lots of priests with no suitable church, I went to see Professor Giovanni Carandente, the 1990 Biennale director. He had a passion for sculpture, especially outdoor installations, but instead of a remote piazza, he suggested several sites *inside* the prestigious official Gardini itself.

'Then suddenly he leaned towards me across his huge mahogany desk, "The Esedra!" he announced.

'I was stunned. The Esedra is a vast space right in the very centre of the Venice Biennale Giardini. Curators would kill for less. Thus overnight I became a curator and commissioner, and two years later

Demarco's idea came to fruition with "Scotland at the Venice Biennale 1990" centre stage, the envy of all!

'On the day a bagpiper serenaded the three artists: Kate Whiteford, David Mach and Arthur Watson, who represented Scotland, and – bagpipes always a draw – we all subsequently appeared in press photos worldwide as well as on numerous European TV stations.

'Carandente was delighted. His beloved Biennale had got off to a flying start. Richard Demarco took it all in his stride.

'As usual, Ricky had the initial idea. Let others make it work!'

4

There shall be an Edinburgh Festival!

THIS WAS ROMEO AND JULIET AT CRAIGMILLAR CASTLE
Richard Demarco presents BOX HEDGE Theatres
production of SHAKESPEARE'S MASTERPIECE
in collaboration with CRAIGMILLAR FESTIVAL
society

EDINBURGH FESTIVAL   R. DEMARCO

THIS WAS AN UNIQUE PRODUCTION BECAUSE IT WAS
A DEMARCO FESTIVAL Theatre PRODUCTION IN COLLABORATION
WITH THE CRAIGMILLAR FESTIVAL'S DIRECTOR — HELEN CRUMMY!

Primroses at Dalmeny

AS SUBSTANTIAL LANDOWNERS on the outskirts of the City, it was only to be expected that the Rosebery family should be in on the start of the Edinburgh Festival of 1947. In those mid-20th century days elitism was afforded a far more munificent status than it commands today, more is the pity for it is elitism and patronage that invariably sponsors, creates and perpetuates great art.

To begin with, Harry, sixth Earl of Rosebery, briefly Secretary of State for Scotland, had two years earlier been appointed Chairman of the fledgling Scottish Tourist Board and it was only natural his talented wife Countess Eva, with their influential contacts in the international cultural world, should be invited to become a member of the committee set up to explore the possibilities of launching a Festival of the Arts in Edinburgh.

Dismayed at the exorbitant cost of seeding a feasibility plan, the committee were on the point of abandoning the whole crazy project until Lady Rosebery handed them a lifeline, the winnings from *Ocean Swell*, her husband's 1944 Derby winning racehorse.

Thus was cemented the Edinburgh Festival's close relationship with the historic Primrose family of Dalmeny House and Barnbougle Castle at South Queensferry.

Now there will be some who might consider Primrose an unlikely Scottish surname, but it actually originates from the lands of Primrose in Dunfermline, appearing first in a mid-12th century charter. An early ancestor was Jonne Prymros, a stone mason from Culross who in 1387 was contracted to work on St Giles Parish Church. Another was James Primrose, Clerk to the Privy Council under James VI & I.

In 1662, Archibald Primrose purchased the Barony of Barnbougle and Dalmeny and moved himself and his family into the 13th-century tower house which stands to this day. Following Scotland's European connections, Archibald's youngest son fought with the Imperial Army in Hungary during the reign of James VII and II. In 1703, he was created Earl of Rosebery in Queen Anne's Coronation Honours.

As the Primrose family prospered politically, so did their domestic aspirations expand and the English architect William Wilkins was commissioned in 1817 to begin work on Dalmeny House. It was the first Tudor-revival house to be built in Scotland.

Having served in various ministerial posts under the British Prime Minister William Ewart Gladstone's Whig government, the fifth Earl succeeded him as Prime Minister in 1894. With his marriage to the fabulously wealthy Hannah Rothschild, he and his wife divided their time between their Scottish and English homes, the Gothic-style Dalmeny House in Midlothian and Mentmore Towers in Buckinghamshire. With the death of the sixth Earl in 1974, Mentmore Towers was sold and many of the treasures of the Rothschild Collection were brought to Dalmeny, which was opened to the public in 1979.

Probably the most impressive collection on display is to be found in the room dedicated to Napoleon Bonapart. This features the most comprehensive accumulation of Napoleonic memorabilia to be found outside of France. The multi-talented fifth Earl was fascinated by the Emperor and wrote his biography. Exhibits include portraits: Napoleon's throne as First Consul, his shaving stand from the Palais de Compiegne, his desk, his chair when in exile on the Isle of St Helena, and the pillow upon which the Emperor's head rested after death.

When Neil, seventh Earl of Rosebery inherited the title and estate in 1974, he and his wife Deirdre continued the family's prolific engagement with the arts in Scotland, to some degree through Neil Rosebery's Northern Light Stage and Technical Services Company. Their son Lord Dalmeny is Chairman of Sotheby's, Auctioneers and succeeded to the earldom on the death of his father in June 2024..

In 1972, the foreshore of the Dalmeny estate, as part of that year's EDINBURGH ARTS programme, became part of a lively expedition from Cramond to South Queensferry.

...and 'Let the People Sing!'

The concept began with a mother, daughter of an accomplished musician, asking the headmaster of the local primary school if her son Philip could have violin lessons and she was refused. This simple rejection prompted Helen Crummy to organise a community arts project which went on to win international acclaim for using arts as the catalyst for social caring and social change.

Remarkable results can be achieved through the arts but it takes a special kind of determined human being to make things happen.

Helen Crummy was born a 'Leither', the eldest of six children but in 1931, her family were among the first residents of Craigmillar. Married in 1942 to Larry Crummy, a soldier with the Durham Light Infantry, the couple set up home in Greendykes on the edge of Craigmillar on the east side of Edinburgh and had three sons, the youngest of which is the talented Andrew Crummy, designer of the Great Tapestry of Scotland.

Post Second World War, Craigmillar and Niddrie had become a neglected Edinburgh suburb centred on the ruins of an old abandoned royal castle. However, the one thing all such marginalised places invariably have in common is a deeply entrenched community spirit.

Early on, Helen had launched a mothers' club, forming a self-help group for local women. In 1962, she and members of the community including local councillor Jack Kane, who went on to become Lord Provost of Edinburgh in 1971, launched the Craigmillar Festival Society.

Where some only saw deprivation and endemic poverty, Helen saw opportunity. Harnessing local talent, she persuaded her neighbours to write and produce their own musicals and plays. Employing 600 people, 1,500 volunteers, over 17,000 individuals either attended or took part in the annual event. An accomplished writer herself, in 1992 she wrote the bestselling *Let the People Sing!: Story of Craigmillar.*

Who would have believed that under the patronage and guidance of Richard Demarco in collaboration with Helen Crummy, the Box Hedge Theatre Company directed by Anthony Lilley would in 1997 perform William Shakespeare's *Romeo and Juliet* at Craigmillar Castle to a full house during the Craigmillar Festival?

Over 40 years, the Craigmillar Festival prospered until 2002 when it was rebranded as the Craigmillar & Niddrie Community Festival. It continues under that name. Helen Crummy was awarded an MBE in 1972 and died in 2011. In 2014, Richard Demarco and the journalist Ruth Wishart unveiled a statue of Helen created by Tim Chalk outside the East Neighbourhood Centre on Niddrie Mains Road.

Among the Craigmillar Festival Society's more controversial commissions in 1976 was a sculpture from Jimmy Boyle of Gulliver, the 'Gentle Giant who Shares and Cares'. This was unveiled by Billy Connolly and was the longest concrete sculpture in Europe. It was described at the time by Boyle as 'a symbol of that particular period when disadvantaged communities were for the first time demanding to be heard.'

In 2006, it was deemed necessary to reroute the Niddrie Burn which passed straight through the statue and, being less than 30 years old, the order was given for it to be demolished. Only the left foot with indented toes was saved.

5

Collision course

NUMBER 8 MELVILLE CRESCENT, HOUSED THE DEMARCO GALLERY FROM 1966 UNTIL 1973 — SEVEN EVENTFUL YEARS IN A WELL-NIGH PERFECT, ELEGANT NEW TOWN HOUSE

IN 1970 THIS GALLERY HOUSED AN EXHIBITION ENTITLED 'NEW DIRECTIONS'

NEW DIRECTIONS' WAS A COMPREHENSIVE EXHIBITION OF THE AVANT-GARDE IN SCOTLAND AND —A RESPONSE TO THE ELECTRIFYING ARTISTS WORKING BEYOND THE ZEITGEIST OF THE WORLDBRIDGE

3 ROMANIAN ARTISTS HORIA BERNEA PAUL NEAGU & IDE PAVEL

A SCOTTISH ARTISTS WHO EXHIBITED PAT DOUTHWAITE ALISTAIR PARK MARGARET MELLIS JOCHERY

GEORGE OLIVER
—SCOTTISH ARTIST-PHOTOGRAPHER—

STEFAN WEWERKA

GUNTHER UECKER

LESLEY BEYNON—GALLERY ASSISTANT

GUNTHER UECKER AND STEFAN WERE TWO GERMAN ARTISTS EXHIBITING IN THE OFFICIAL EDINBURGH FESTIVAL EXHIBITION WITH THE PALINDROMIC TITLE OF → S T R A T E G Y — G E T — A R T S ←
THE TITLE WAS AN ARTWORK IN ITSELF BY THE SWISS ARTIST, ANDRE MOMKINS→STRATEGY-GET-ARTS & WAS PRESENTED AT EDINBURGH COLLEGE OF ART BECAUSE 35 ARTISTS WERE INVOLVED

CORDELIA OLIVER SUB CARA LINE

Barlinnie and Beuys

After many years in prison, I was allowed a day out. This was
1974. I stepped through the small opening of the remarkable
Poorhouse doors. Joseph Beuys and Buckminster Fuller
were speaking. It was a memorable event. Those of us who
experienced it should be grateful to Ricky Demarco for having
had the vision and courage to present it. These people made
art an experience to be cherished.

In essence, the esteem in which I hold Joseph Beuys is
conveyed through my actions on that day in 1974. He is
the only person who could have drawn me into the dark,
Dickensian surroundings of the Poorhouse after many years
in prison. To put this into its proper perspective, I did have to
return to my prison cell in a few hours.

Jimmy Boyle, *Cencrastus,* 2005

2024 MARKED THE 50th anniversary of the day when Richard
Demarco introduced Jimmy Boyle to Joseph Beuys. This meeting
took place in the Demarco Gallery's Forrest Hill Poorhouse during
the 1974 Edinburgh International Festival programme that Richard
had devised. He had invited Beuys to collaborate with the American
polymath Buckminster Fuller, who embodied the spirit of avant-garde
thinking in the both the arts and sciences.

Together for a six-hour-long example of what became known as
'performance art', they provided incontrovertible proof that Scotland
could not have a long-term future if it committed itself to using a
non-renewable source of energy in the form of what was the birth
of industry known as North Sea oil. There is an 8mm film recording
of the exact words used by Boyle when Richard introduced him to
Beuys. Boyle introduced himself with the words 'I am the Coyote',
referring to the fact that Joseph Beuys had visited New York with
the intention of having a conversation, not with President Richard
Nixon but with the despised 'Coyote', regarded by human beings as
beneath contempt.

Richard invited Jimmy Boyle to write a statement for a special
edition of the Scottish journal *Cencrastus* under the editorship of
Raymond Ross and the guest editorship of Steve Robb. This edition

was subtitled 'Joseph Beuys in Scotland'. It was published to celebrate the fact that the Tate Gallery under the curatorship of Sean Rainbird had, in 2004, honoured Beuys with a major exhibition within the hallowed walls of Tate Modern.

Little did Richard realise that his conversations with Joseph Beuys in the early 1970s would lead to a confrontation with the Scottish Arts Council which represented the official Government world controlling, with a heavy hand, the cultural life of Scotland. He well remembers the questions he put to Beuys and his immediate responses. Richard simply asked him 'When you say that everyone is an artist, does that include those unfortunates who find themselves in prison?'

His reply was immediate: 'Ja, of course.'

Richard's second question was, 'Does that include prisoners serving life sentences?'

Beuys replied, 'Of course.'

Richard's third question was 'Does that include murderers?' He replied 'Ja, ja.'

Then Richard said, 'I do know that you don't wish to waste your time; therefore, I strongly suggest that you should visit what I consider to be an important experiment in penal reform, by visiting a prison within a prison. I am thinking of the Special Unit within the Victorian walls of a notorious prison in Glasgow known as Her Majesty's Prison Barlinnie.'

This was at a time when the Demarco Gallery was housed on the Royal Mile in Edinburgh's Old Town, in a historic building known as Monteith House. When Joseph Beuys gladly stood in for Jimmy Boyle at Jimmy Boyle's exhibition entitled, 'In Defence of the Innocent', Richard knew that Joseph Beuys had begun an enduring friendship with deep respect for the fact that, against all the odds, Jimmy Boyle was proving to be a highly creative sculptor and a wordsmith of exceptional talent. His A Sense of Freedom was published by Canongate, then newly founded by Angus and Stephanie Wolf Murray. It proved to be a bestseller.

After seven years of exemplary behaviour as a distinctly creative human being, Joseph Beuys found Jimmy Boyle in a distressed state, having learned that he was to be removed from the Special Unit and handcuffs once again placed on his wrists. He was to spend his remaining years of imprisonment, far from the Special Unit, in the restricted environment known as Edinburgh's Saughton Prison. Joseph Beuys was heading for Edinburgh to take part in the Demarco Gallery's official Edinburgh Festival exhibition celebrating the tenth anniversary of 'Strategy: Get Arts'.

Little did Joseph Beuys, or indeed Richard, know that, in the first week of the Edinburgh International Festival, The Scottish Arts Council would call an emergency meeting with the Board of the Demarco Gallery. This was in response to the legal action made by Joseph Beuys in the form of a letter to the Secretary of State for Scotland, making clear that, as far as he was concerned, Jimmy Boyle's life in the Special Unit must be regarded as a complete success and that, indeed, he had given to himself the freedom that all artists embody when they provide proof that their art is about an expression of freedom.

Richard has been unable to forget the words used as an indictment of what was the official contribution made to the Edinburgh International Festival by the Demarco Gallery. These words were addressed to him in his role as Artistic Director. They made it clear that the Scottish Arts Council's annual grant was to be removed forthwith, leaving the funding for the exhibition dependent on that which had been given by the City of Düsseldorf, the German Embassy in London and The Goethe-Institut in Scotland.

The words still ring in his ears – 'You have brought dishonour to the meaning of art. You have brought dishonour to the meaning of art in Scotland. You have brought dishonour to the Richard Demarco Gallery.'

This meant that somehow, since that fateful year of 1980, he had to continue his self-appointed task of helping to internationalise the cultural life of Scotland without the essential guarantee of any annual Scottish Government financial support.

Richard's first ever meeting between Joseph Beuys and Jimmy Boyle had taken place in what had been, since the Middle Ages, a notorious equivalent in Scotland of London's Bethlem Royal Hospital, known as Bedlam, England's first asylum. It was known as the Forrest Hill Poorhouse. It suffered from a leaking temporary roof and from a lack of normal civilising amenities.

However, in 1974 it proved to be the ideal place for the Richard Demarco Gallery's experiment in education through the arts. It was here that Jimmy Boyle introduced himself to Joseph Beuys with the telling words – 'Hello, Professor Beuys. I am the Coyote.' He did so because he had just seen an exhibition in the Forrest Hill Poorhouse of photographs taken by Caroline Tisdall, the art critic of *The Guardian*.

These photographs were a unique artistic statement which took place in New York in the gallery of René Block. This gallery had been converted to contain the cage in which Joseph Beuys could be in fruitful dialogue with a coyote over a period of three consecutive days. Richard considers this as a nodal point in the history of the Edinburgh Festival. Joseph Beuys entitled this poetic 'action' as 'I like America and America likes me'.

Richard considers himself fortunate to have this historic moment filmed on a Super 8 camera by Howard Walker. He had accompanied Bill Beech, an artist that he relied upon to conduct an experiment in art education within the walls of the Forrest Hill Poorhouse in collaboration with his fellow sculptors, Phil Hitchcock, of the Chicago Art Institute, and Steve Whitacre and his colleague Michael Miles from the Kansas Art Institute. They effectively strengthened performance art in the Demarco Gallery's Festival's exhibitions programme and, at the same time, honoured the outstanding work of the Special Unit.

They had proved themselves, not only fully engaged in the life of the Special Unit in the Poorhouse, but also in the Special Unit itself. Thankfully, Howard Walker's film footage still exists as proof that this most unlikely cultural and academic dialogue is identified with the history of the Edinburgh International Festival.

Of course, all this was made possible under the aegis of the Demarco Gallery's Edinburgh Arts experiment in education through the language of all the arts. It was the ideal language to involve fellow inmates of the Special Unit, particularly the poet Larry Winters and the sculptor Hugh Collins who had gained recognition for his writings, just as Jimmy Boyle had gained his freedom through his outstanding gifts in the world of literature.

To celebrate the 50th anniversary of the Edinburgh Festival in 1996, Professor George Steiner delivered a thought-provoking lecture. This took place at Edinburgh University's prestigious McEwan Hall. He referred to the fact that the Edinburgh Festival needed to have a distinct academic dimension.

The Forrest Hill Poorhouse still exists as a garden adjoining what is now defined as luxury flats. Its walls are still abutting the graveyard of Greyfriars Kirk, the world of 'Greyfriars Bobby', the loyal Scots terrier who honoured his master. When Joseph Beuys collaborated with Buckminster Fuller in a six-hour-long 'action', questioning the decision by Scotland's politicians to commit Scotland's economic growth to North Sea oil as a non-renewable energy resource, he created a work of art in which he likened the image of Greyfriars Bobby to be 'the First of the Giants'. This was in reference to a front-page article in a Scottish newspaper that suggested the first of the giants was a gigantic North Sea oil platform.

6

To the sweet flower-soul unfolden

QUOTATIONS FROM A REPORT BY TOM HUDSON, DIRECTOR OF STUDIES CARDIFF COLLEGE OF ART "ONE GROUP CREATED A GREAT BLACK FRIEZE."

DRAWN BY TOM HUDSON CLASSES IN CREATIVE MENTALITY ONE INDOOR - ONE OUTDOOR ON CANDIDO BEACH

TOM HUDSON

"LEGS ASTRIDE AND ARMS RAISED, A GROUP OF 10-12 STARTUSH POLYWENE ACROSS THE BEACH, THE WIND PRESSED THE BLACK HARD AGAINST THEIR BODIES MAKING A REPRODUCTION OF BLACK "WINGED" VICTORIES AND OF COURSE THEY MOVED COLLECTIVELY SWAYING AND TURNING — A BLACK SCULPTURE OF POWER AND DRAMA"

"FOR HE THIRD TIME WE WENT OUT OF THE GALLERY TO CANDIDO BEACH ON THE EDGE OF EARTH, WITH HE TIDE WELL DOWN, REVEALING A VARIETY OF PHYSICAL PHENOMENA: GREAT STRETCHES OF EXPANSE AND THE FOAM

"ONE GROUP BUILT A BEAUTIFUL FOUNTAIN." A HUGE MANDALA OF INTERPENETRATING RODS, SWAYING IN THE WIND FESTOONED WITH LOOPS OF WHITE

RICHARD JOYCE DEMARCO GALLERY ASSISTANT

THE CAUSEWAY, TRIANGULATED PYRAMIDS LEADING TO

STUART HOPPS DEMONSTRATES AN EXERCISE IN THE BLACK DAILY WARMUP

"WHEN I WAS ASKED TO INVOLVE SCOTTISH THEATRE BALLET IN THE EDINBURGH ARTS SUMMER SCHOOL THIS YEAR, WE WERE NATURALLY VERY EXCITED ... I SUGGESTED WE GOT THE SUMMER SCHOOL TO DANCE, AND SAW THE OPPORTUNITY TO PHYSICALLY INVOLVE YOUNG PEOPLE NOT USUALLY INTO BALLET. THEY WOULD EXPLORE CONCEPTS NOT UNFAMILIAR TO THEM - FOAM, STRUCTURE, SPACE, TEXTURE, DESIGN, DYNAMICS." STUART HOPPS.

Craigcrook Castle

CRAIGCROOK CASTLE, SQUATTING on the lower slopes of Corstorphine Hill to the north-west of Edinburgh, was home to the Demarco Archive from 2009 until 2013.

Although 17th century in origin, the building is like many of its kind and a hotch-potch of periodic add-ons ideally suited the ethos of Demarco, especially as it was from here that the *Edinburgh Review* emanated, a periodical in which the French writer Marie-Henri Beyle, under the pen-name Stendhal, wrote 'I have dined with a handsome and charming young man – a face of 18, though the age of 28, the profile of an angel, the gentlest of manners ...When this young man enters an English drawing room, all of the women immediately depart. He is the greatest poet living.'

In response, George Gordon, Lord Byron, an 'Englishman sometimes considered to be a Scotsman,' wrote *English Bards and Scotch Reviewers: A Satyre* in which he observed 'It would indeed require a Herculese to crush the Hydra.'

An early occupant of Craigcrook Castle had been William Adamson who was killed at the Battle of Pinkie in 1547. Sir John Hall of Dunglass who became Lord Provost of Edinburgh took up residence in 1669. On the death of a later owner, John Strachan ws, in 1719, the property was handed over to the Craigcrook Mortification Charitable Trust which hands out donations to the impoverished elderly.

Following the tenancy of Archibald Constable, the publisher, in 1815, the castle was occupied by Lord Jeffrey, a contemporary of Sir Walter Scott. A Lord Advocate at the Court of Session, he became member of Parliament for Perth burghs, and it was he who published the *Edinburgh Review*. His ghost is said to walk the corridors.

So much of the joy of occupying such places is the sense of the passing of time. In town to edit the *Edinburgh News*, the English poet Gerald Massey, was sufficiently impressed.

> *Craigcrook Roses! ruby, golden,*
> *Glowing gorgeous; faint with passion;*
> *To the sweet flower-soul unfolden;*
> *Wreath me in the old Greek fashion.*
> *Queen of sweetness, crowned in splendour,*

Every rich bound bud encloses;
Yet so meek and womanly tender.
Are you Royal Craigcrook roses,
Warm and windy Craigcrook roses.

Celebrated for its literary salons throughout the Victorian era, Craigcrook Castle played host to, among others, Charles Dickens, Hans Christian Andersen, George Eliot and Alfred Lord Tennyson. It was therefore ideal to provide a momentary retreat for the 2,500 artworks, including paintings, prints, drawings and sculptures and 20,000 multilingual publications of the Demarco Archive. In the words of Lord Byron, 'There are four questions of value in life, Don Octavio. What is sacred? Or what is the spirit made? What is worth living for and what is worth dying for? The answer to each is the same. Only love.'

At Craigcrook Castle, a room was devoted to the art works that Joseph Beuys made during his eight visits to Scotland between 1970 and 1981. In this room was evidence of Beuys's botanical drawings and paintings juxtaposed with a set of three flower studies by Rory McEwen in memory of that extraordinary journey Richard Demarco, Joseph Beuys and Rory McEwen made to Rannoch Moor on 13 August 1970.

Priestfield

In medieval times, the south-eastern slopes of today's Holyrood Park, then known simply as Priestfield, were owned by a colony of Cistercian monks from Northumberland. Their tenure came to an end when their possessions were handed over to the Scottish Crown during the Scottish Wars of Independence. Thereafter, the lands of Priestfield were eventually acquired by Walter Chepman, printer to James IV, who passed them on to the earls of Haddington.

Around 1670, the estate was sold to James Dick, a wealthy merchant trader who served as the city's Dean of Guild. In 1679, he became Lord Provost of the City and during his term as First Citizen, with a town house in the Lawnmarket, he instructed for the streets of the city to be cleaned at his own expense, to remove the waste as fertiliser for his estate. It is hard to imagine such municipal benevolence nowadays.

But this was an age of rumbling religious dissent and the Dicks were of Roman Catholic persuasion. In 1681, the year James Dick was elected Member of Parliament for Edinburgh, Priestfield House was burned to the ground during a student anti-Catholic riot. Unperturbed, Dick, who was to purchase a Nova Scotia baronetcy in 1707, commissioned the architect Sir William Bruce to build him a distinctive new home. He renamed it Prestonfield to distance it from its previous priestly associations.

No expense was spared. Interiors were lavishly decorated with exotic plasterwork from Italian artisans who had previously worked at the Palace of Holyrood. Tooled and gilded leather wall coverings were imported from Córdoba, Spain. Tapestries, Chinoiserie lacquer cabinets and fine Dutch paintings were purchased. All of these extravagances remain to this day.

On his death in 1728, the Prestonfield estate passed to his daughter's grandson William Cunynghame who, assuming the baronetcy and incorporating the Dick surname, passed both on to his brother Alexander.

Having travelled extensively in Italy with his friend the painter Allan Ramsay, Alexander commissioned the Norrie family of decorative painters, father and two sons, to create Italian-style landscapes on the panelling of the dining room. The American statesman Benjamin Franklin, the philosopher David Hume, Doctor Samuel Johnson and his biographer James Boswell were among those whom Alexander and his wife entertained here.

Moving on through the generations, Prestonfield continued to be occupied by the Dick-Cunynghams. A neo-classical porch was added to the house in the early 19th century by the architect James Gillespie Graham with reception rooms and a fine stable block. Then in 1959, the entrepreneurial Captain Anthony Stevenson, who was leasing Seton Palace at Longniddrie from Wemyss Estates, decided to launch a boutique hotel. With Highland cattle roaming the parkland, peacocks on the lawn and a growing reputation for fine cuisine, Prestonfield rapidly became Edinburgh's top gourmet retreat.

James Thomson was only 20 in 1979 when he opened his first restaurant The Witchery on Castlehill, swiftly followed by The Secret Garden. Then in 2003, he acquired Prestonfield.

He admits to having been in love with the hotel from the age of five and he had returned to work there while studying at college. 'I embarked upon a multi-million-pound refurbishment of the historic interiors,' he explained. 'I wanted to create a bold alternative to some of Edinburgh's bland uniform hotels.'

James has most certainly succeeded in doing just this, earning him a string of accolades – the award of Hotelier of the Year, and an OBE. More recently he has been appointed a Deputy Lord Lieutenant of Edinburgh. Thanks to his immense generosity there is a forthcoming event to be held to raise funds for The Demarco Archive Trust.

Cramond

Archaeological excavation has uncovered lost evidence of habitation at Cramond as far back as 8500BC, making it the earliest known human settlement in Scotland. The Romans, who arrived in the following millennium, must also have recognised this strategic location on the mouth of the River Almond in the Firth of Forth. Under orders from the Emperor Antoninus Pius, a substantial fort was erected to guard the eastern approaches of the Antonine Wall.

A rectangular site, uncovered in 1954, occupied over five acres with a harbour. Shards of pottery and coins featuring the heads of the Emperor Antoninus and Emperor Septimius Severus suggest Roman occupancy up until 211. It was also established that Cramond's medieval parish church was situated within the fort's boundaries, as was a section of Cramond House.

A stone altar found in the gardens of Cramond House was inscribed with the Latin words MATRIBALA TERVIS ET MATRIB CAM PESTRICoH TNGp INS VCP SNM OIRs XXVV. This translates as a dedication to 'The Alatervan Mothers and the Mothers of the Parade Ground.' Nevertheless, historians have squabbled over its provenance ever since.

What proved to be infinitely more consequential is the Cramond Lioness discovered in the harbour 1997 by a local boatman tasked with rowing back and forth across the mouth of the River Almond transporting tourists and locals between Cramond Foreshore and Dalmeny (House) estate. This is a lump of sandstone carved into the shape of a lioness devouring a male figure and is now resident in the Museum of Scotland in Chambers Street, Edinburgh. In contrast, there is a giant Eagle Rock standing 100 yards from the former boatman's cottage to the west overlooking Cramond Island.

In the centuries following the Roman departure from Scotland, Cramond was occupied by the Votadini, an Iron Age tribe who spoke a Brythonic Celtic language from whence the name Caer Amon, meaning 'Fort on the River', derives. Nearby, lands were used as royal hunting grounds from the time of David I, hence the modern day 'King's Cramond' designation, not to mention the Knights Templar and modern day 'Templar's Cramond.'

A tower, now known as Cramond Tower, was built to accommodate Bishops of Dunkeld, to whose diocese it belonged in the early 15th century. Cramond was incorporated into the City of Edinburgh in 1920. From Cramond Beach, a tidal causeway stretches one mile across to Cramond Island owned by Rosebery Estates. Unsuspecting visitors have often been known to become stranded there by the incoming tide.

Offshore is Inchcolm Island, Columba's Island, allegedly visited by St Columba in 567. By the 12th century a Priory, then an Abbey, was built and occupied by Augustinian monks. Most notable among them was Walter Bower, who was Abbot from 1418–89 and responsible for the 16 book *Scotichronichon*, Scotland's most significant historic book of reference.

Like the neighbouring islands of Inchkeith and the Isle of May, Inchcolm came frequently under attack, early on from the Danes and in later centuries from English raiders.

Much has already been written, , not least in *Demarco's Edinburgh*, about the groundbreaking productions of Shakespeare's *Macbeth*, directed by Johnny Bett and La Zattera di Babele theatre under a darkening sky on Inchcolm during the Edinburgh Festivals of 1988 and 1989.

Suffice it to say that these productions were triumphant spectacles of thrilling, open air theatrical experience.

To the east along the wondrous southern shoreline of the Firth of Forth from Cramond Beach, affording spectacular panoramic views of the three-mile-long Silverknowes Beach and Promenade walkway, stands the indomitable Eddie Tait's Boardwalk Beach Club, a favourite stop-off location for walkers and marathon runners, and ideal location for book launches, music events and art and photography exhibitions.

It was on a dog walk with friends that Eddie noticed that a former toilet block on the beach was up for sale and much to his wife Sarah's concern (and later praise), raced to acquire it. Eddie and his family are proud locals. His uncles helped to found the Silverknowes Golf Club back in 1956, captained Davidson's Mains Primary School and local football teams, and his cousin was Davidson's Mains Gala Queen. Eddie had enjoyed summers playing in the grounds of Lauriston Castle. In his final year at the Royal High School he was made Chief Executive of the school's Young Enterprise Company, and it was at Napier University that he first met his Scottish business hero Sir Tom Farmer, founder of Kwik-Fit, and later owner of Hibernian Football Club.

With a guided notion towards business studies, Eddie qualified from the University of Edinburgh with an Honours Business Degree. At Heriot Watt University, he gained a Masters degree in International Banking and Finance before joining Morgan Stanley at Canary Wharf in London where, 'seemingly a life time ago', he founded the Scots in London social network.

'Richard Demarco is the personification of a paradox,' Eddie observed. 'He says he is not commercial but he has sold over 5,000 of his own drawings and paintings. He has been honoured by seven European countries and seven universities, yet he is not widely celebrated in his own country among the young as he should be.

'He travelled behind the Iron Curtain more than 60 times but he is more comfortable in the historic settings of Celtic Scotland and introducing poets and engineers to the coastline of the British Isles. Admittedly he has been given The Edinburgh Award but has been pushed from pillar to post around the city as he fell in and out of favour with the so-called establishment, possibly because his name and brand have been synonymous with the Edinburgh Festival, Edinburgh and Scotland, and the wider European Arts Scene, which makes the establishment with its own agendas uncomfortable.

'Mentally he remains as sharp as a tack and still goes on and on with boundless enthusiasm about his passions and his causes and he still needs to be reeled back when his net catches are overstretched.'

Lauriston Castle

On the north-west side of Scotland's capital are the characterful turrets of Lauriston Castle. Overlooking the Firth of Forth and Cramond Island, the early importance of this tranquil, strategic site in Scotland's defences is almost forgotten.

A castle stood here in medieval times but was largely destroyed during the first Earl of Hertford's 'Rough Wooing' of 1544. This was a ruthless attempt to bully the Scottish nobility into signing a treaty to marry off the two-year-old Mary Queen of Scots to the seven-year-old Prince Edward of England. When the Scots remained ambivalent to the plan, Henry VIII's brother-in-law and military commander, later created Duke of Somerset, invaded and ravaged all in his path.

Those were dangerous, terrible times for the south of Scotland when the flames engulfing Edinburgh and the Abbey of Holyrood continued for three days.

Virtually everything that can be seen at Lauriston Castle today therefore dates from 50 years after that devastating period in Scottish history. In 1590, Sir Archibald Napier, seventh Laird of Merchiston and father of John Napier, best known for devising logarithms, rebuilt the remains of the original fortress into a tower house for his younger son, also Archibald. What he created initially was a four-storey, stone L-Plan tower house, with a circular stair tower, with two-storey angle turrets complete with gun loops.

Thereafter, the fortunes of the Napiers, like all great Scottish families, rose and fell, and the property changed hands regularly over the following centuries, being early on occupied by the father of the extraordinary John Law (1671–1729), a gambler who established the Banque Générale in France, issued the first banknotes in Europe and precipitated France's economic collapse.

In the 19th century, Thomas Allen, a mineralogist who became a banker, commissioned the distinguished Scottish architect William Burn to add on a Jacobean extension. Allen died in Northumberland, but by then the Lauriston estate had been passed on to Lord Rutherford of Crosshill (1791–1852), an advocate who became Member of Parliament for Leith Burghs, which lay almost on his doorstep.

Thomas Crawfurd, eighth Baron Cartsburn acquired the property in 1871 and made several improvements, but in 1902 it was bought by

William Reid, an Edinburgh-based cabinet manufacturer who installed plumbing and electricity and filled the interiors with art and fine furniture. In 1905 a stone carving of an astrological horoscope was discovered and placed on an outer wall on the south-west corner.

In 1926, the castle was bequeathed to the people of Scotland on the understanding that its contents remained intact. Since then it has been lovingly administered as a museum and wedding venue by the City of Edinburgh Council.

The Reids were avid collectors of all kinds of decorative treasures and among the items on display, amid sumptuous surroundings judged to be typical of an Edwardian manor house, are fine pieces of Italian furniture, Sheffield Plate, Crossley Wool mosaics and Blue John from Derbyshire. A tour of the castle in the 21st century takes visitors through the principal rooms: John Reid's practically designed Study and through to the elegant Drawing Room, Dining Room, Library, and Kitchen, the latter providing an interesting contrast between life 'upstairs' and 'downstairs'.

Lauriston Castle is set within an elegant garden laid out by William Henry Playfair during the 1840s. In 2002, a Japanese garden was introduced, designed by Takashi Sawano, a Japanese landscape architect who has been living and designing Japanese gardens in the West for many years. Conceived as a 'Friendship Garden' it was gifted by the people of Kyoto, the former Imperial Capital of Japan. To the rear are three croquet lawns laid out between 1950 and 1955, and much enjoyed by members of the Edinburgh Croquet Club. On the eastern side are woodland walks amid mature examples of monkey puzzle trees. In the summer, the grounds are ablaze with the colours of the adjacent bluebell wood.

Richard Demarco has led innumerable Edinburgh art students to be inspired not only by the contents of Lauriston Castle but also by the panoramic landscape that it provides of the Firth of Forth shorelines both of Midlothian and the Kingdom of Fife.

7

Edinburgh's first sculpture park

THE BURNING OF 'LOCAL HERO' TOOK PLACE IN BLACKFRIARS STREET BEFORE THE GALLERY-GOERS WHO HAD BEEN INVITED TO ATTEND THE OPENING OF THE GALLERY'S FESTIVAL EXHIBITION

THE ELEMENTAL FORCES OF FIRE AND WATER WERE CONJOINED

THE UMBRELLA INDICATES THE ACTION TOOK PLACE IN A DOWNPOUR OF RAIN

THE MAKING OF THE SCULPTURE (PORTRAYED BY DAVID MACH TOGETHER WITH THE BRONZE "THE BUTTON" WHICH BURNED [?]) WAS PART OF KINGSTON UNIVERSITY'S CONTRIBUTION TO THE 1992 DEMARCO GALLERY EDINBURGH FESTIVAL EXHIBITION ENTITLED "PERPENDICULAR PLUS"

ROBERT MACH

DAVID MACH

'LOCAL HERO' WAS THE NAME GIVEN BY DAVID MACH TO HIS SCULPTURE MADE OF THOUSANDS OF MATCHES. BY THE PROCESS OF SETTING IT ALIGHT, THE BRIGHTLY COLOURED HEAD WAS ENVELOPED IN FLAMES FOR A FEW MINUTES THEN EMERGED A BLACKENED MASK, REMINISCENT OF AFRICAN MASKS. IT WAS A PORTRAIT OF MYSELF AS I ENDED MY DAYS AS DIRECTOR OF THE DEMARCO GALLERY IN BLACKFRIARS STREET

— Richard DEMARCO

Hopetoun House

NO DOUBT IT was a semblance of fate that the second Earl of Harewood, second Director of the Edinburgh Festival, Charles, third Marquess of Linlithgow who had inherited Hopetoun House at South Queensferry, and the painter Earl Haig who owned Bemersyde in the Scottish Borders, were all three captured by the German Army during the Second World War and held as Prisoners-of-War at Colditz Castle in Saxony.

All three of these great men were possessed of outstanding integrity and courage and shared a similar European sensitivity regardless of the atrocities of Nazi Germany they witnessed first-hand. All three men were fully in step with the healing message of that first Edinburgh Festival of the Arts in 1947.

There can be little doubt it that it was these qualities which opened their eyes to the infinite possibilities of creative freedom. Needless to say, there was an instant rapport with the younger Richard Demarco who inspirationally seized the opportunities to celebrate the hinterlands they occupied.

With its all-embracing wings looming up as you approach along its substantial park, the frontal range of Hopetoun House lies a mile or so distance from the medieval ferry town of South Queensferry. Both coming and going, there are spectacular views across the Firth of Forth towards the Kingdom of Fife. This is a house that was built to impress.

The history of the Hopetoun estate is also tantalising. A fortified castle existed on the original Abercorn estate as early as the 12th century when it was held by Sir William de Graham, ancestor of the dukes of Montrose.

At Abercorn, on the estate, stands Midhope Castle. This was built c1458 by John Martin who had also acquired Carden Castle, a deer park in Fife, and holds a certain nostalgic sentiment for Roddy Martine since John was a distant relative. Sold to Henry Livingstone in 1478, Midhope was rebuilt by Alexander Drummond in 1587 then significantly remodelled by George, third Earl of Livingstone in 1664.

Today, Midhope will be familiar to enthusiasts of the STARZ historical television series *Outlander* since it serves as the fictional site of Lallybroch (Broch Tuarach), ancestral home of the drama's handsome hero Jamie Fraser, played by Sam Heughan from Dumfriesshire. At the time of going to press, plans are allegedly afoot to transform the site into a distillery and visitor centre.

The Hope family purchased the Abercorn estate in the mid-17th century and were a remarkably fortunate, acute and prolific dynasty. Their story emerges in the 15th century with John Hope, a Burgess of Edinburgh with trading interests in continental Europe.

John's grandson Thomas was born in Leith 1573 and studied law, rising to become King's Advocate in 1626. Of his four sons, two became judges at the Court of Session, the third was appointed cupbearer to the King and the fourth, Sir James (1614–61), became Master of the Mint and a Lord of Session. Sir James was the first to style himself 'of Hopetoun' taking the old name of Leadhills in Lanarkshire which had come into his possession through marriage to its heiress Anne Foulis. He then set off to the Low Countries to gain an expertise hitherto unknown in Scotland and from which he later extended the family's commercial interests into West Lothian. Lead mining is the basis of the Hope family's prosperity.

In 1678, James's son John (1650–82) purchased the lands of Abercorn on the southern shore of the Firth of Forth from the fourth Earl of Winton and renamed his estate 'Hopetoun'. Alas, he soon after was drowned in the shipwreck of HMS *Gloucester* whilst accompanying the Duke of York, later James VII/II, on a journey to Scotland.

John is said to have given up his seat in the rescue boat to save the future monarch. As a result, his widow, Lady Margaret Hamilton, was left with their two young sons to oversee the emerging mansion house under the instruction of the great Scottish architect Sir William Bruce. On his coming of age in 1703, the same year the first building work was completed, Charles, the eldest son, was created Earl of Hopetoun by Queen Anne, a nod to his father's sacrifice.

Sir William Bruce's original designs for Hopetoun House followed the Italian style introduced into England earlier that same century – a central pile connected by curved colonnades with forward-standing pavilions. The existing west front survives as an admirably restrained and balanced composition.

A zealous supporter of the Act of Union between Scotland and England, the Earl was a man of cultivated tastes who, with his substantial inheritance, set out to copy the splendour of contemporary English country houses. There can be no doubt he had a strong influence on the alterations, enlargement and additions introduced 20 years later by his family's friends, those other iconic Scottish architects, William Adam and subsequently William's son Robert.

The second Earl added to the family holdings by purchasing the Ormiston estates in East Lothian, and was one of the first Governors of Edinburgh Infirmary. The third Earl concentrated on improving his agricultural interests but had no children.

Hopetoun was thus inherited by his half-brother General Sir John Hope who had fought alongside the Duke of Wellington in the Peninsular War. At Hopetoun, he instructed the completion of the State Dining Room and, on one memorable occasion in 1822, entertained George IV to a lunch of turtle soup on the last day of the King's State Visit to Scotland. It is hard to ignore such a dynasty.

Asking for the use of the Earl's sword, King George knighted Captain Adam Ferguson, Keeper of the Regalia in Scotland, and Henry Raeburn, the distinguished Scottish painter, in the Yellow Drawing Room.

John, seventh Earl, was appointed Governor of Victoria and first Governor-General of the Commonwealth of Australia, and was created Marquess of Linlithgow in 1901. Victor, second Marquess, held the office of Viceroy and Governor-General of India from 1936 to 1943. Charles, third Marquess served in the British Army and during the Second World War was captured and imprisoned at Colditz with the 51st Highland Division.

Adrian, fourth Marquess, has enjoyed a successful commercial career in the City of London and today lives quietly on the estate while his son and daughter-in-law Lord and Lady Hopetoun occupy an apartment in the house which, despite it having become a five star visitor attraction, remains very much their private family home.

Lord Hopetoun, a nuclear physicist and software and systems engineer, explains, 'Since 1971, the house and immediate grounds have been owned and run by an independent charitable trust, the Hopetoun House Preservation Trust. Its role is to ensure the future of Hopetoun for public benefit and enjoyment and inspiration through ongoing conservation and education programmes.'

Hopetoun House itself can be seen in seasons one and two of *Outlander* as the home of the fictional Duke of Sandringham. Parts of the house feature as Parisian streets and Jamie and Claire's spare bedroom.

Restoration and conservation are very much at the core of Hopetoun. Within the hallway and rooms open to the public there are innumerable family portraits, fine artefacts, marble busts and items of furniture such as a Genoese mid-18th century gilt wood pier table with its Florentine sample marble top, and a round table in burr oak by William Trotter.

There are paintings by Peter Paul Rubens, Sir Henry Raeburn and Sir Thomas Gainsborough to be seen. Particularly beautiful is the White Satin Bedchamber with its wall hangings; also, the West Ainscot Bedchamber and Ante-Room, and the State Apartments – the Yellow and Red Drawing Rooms and the State Dining Room. The Ballroom in the South Pavilion with its coved plaster ceiling, Aubusson tapestries, chandeliers and a fine chimney piece designed by William Adam, has witnessed many a formal ball and gathering and created so many happy memories.

To precipitate Regency Britain into the 20th century, it was a Richard Demarco Gallery initiative in 1968 to hold an exhibition featuring the works of 34 artists. As part of the EDINBURGH ARTS Edinburgh Festival programme of 1972, it became the Demarco Gallery's Sculpture Park and the shoreline of the Firth of Forth provided the ideal location for The Highland Shakespeare Company's production of Shakespeare's *The Tempest*.

8

A passion for music

THE RESURRECTION

DURING THE EDINBURGH FESTIVAL FRINGE 2022 THERE WAS A CELEBRATORY EXHIBITION IN A TRAQUAIR PAVILION

CATHERINE MAXWELL STEWART PRESENTED AN EXHIBITION IN THE TRAQUAIR HOUSE PAVILIONS

THE EXHIBITION CELEBRATED THE ARTISTS WHO BROUGHT THE EDINBURGH FESTIVAL TO TRAQUAIR — SUCH AS JOANNA PRZYBYLA, PAOLO CAUGO, DERYK HEALEY, KEVIN DAGG, MARY McCUER

THIS EXHIBIT TO CELEBRATED THE 50 YEAR CULTURAL DIALOGUE BETWEEN TRAQUAIR AND THE DEMARCO ARCHIVE

MY FRIENDSHIP WITH PETER & FLORA MAXWELL STUART BEGAN IN THE SIXTIES
THE RESURRECTION IN TRAQUAIR CHAPEL.
16TH CENTURY FLEMISH OAK PANEL — THIS WAS ONE OF THE 2A
PEN & INK AND WATERCOLOURS BY RICHARD DEMARCO ON EXHIBITION AT TRAQUAIR IN 2022

Dalkeith Palace

A HIGH POINT of the Edinburgh International Festival of 2023 was an exhibition of paintings and memorabilia held at Dalkeith Palace, ancestral home of the Dukes of Buccleuch & Queensberry. It was entitled A Passion for Music and was, in essence, about the extraordinary life of someone who might be considered as embodying not only the spirit of the Edinburgh Festival but that vital dimension which emphasises the importance of Scotland's cultural life conjoined with that of Italy, the land of Richard Demarco's Italian forebears.

That exhibition demonstrated that the spirit of the Edinburgh Festival was alive in the 18th and 19th centuries and recreated the world of a unique 18th-century patron of all the arts. She was Lady Elizabeth Montagu, born into a family strongly identified with the cultural life of Regency London. As the wife of Henry, third Duke of Buccleuch, she almost single-handedly promoted an Italo–Scottish cultural dialogue at Dalkeith Palace, and in the drawing rooms of Georgian Edinburgh's burgeoning New Town.

In the summer of 2023, Richard was invited by Charlotte Rostek, Director of Development at Dalkeith Palace, to attend a one-day symposium. A concert in four lessons followed involving 18th-century musical instruments and song. The exhibition was curated by Paul Boucher, the archivist at Boughton House, Northamptonshire, and was the preview for an unforgettable, life-changing exhibition.

Sadly this event coincided with the premature death of the Scottish-born, partly Italian Lady Elizabeth Kerr, Duchess of Buccleuch & Queensberry, who had provided the main source of inspiration for this exhibition which had first been made manifest the year before at the family's English home, Boughton House in Northamptonshire.

Dalkeith Palace is so named for having been where King George IV chose to quarter himself in preference to Holyrood during his historic visit to Scotland in 1822, the first reigning British monarch to set foot in their Scottish realm for over 200 years.

You can virtually drown in the provenance of this remarkable building. A medieval castle existed here from the 12th century when it was held by the de Graham family from whom the barony of Dalkeith in 1342 passed through marriage to the powerful Douglas family. In the mid-15th century, James Douglas of Dalkeith was created Earl of Morton.

In 1503, Henry VIII of England's sister Princess Margaret Tudor, stayed at Dalkeith Castle prior to her arrival in Edinburgh. In 1548, the castle was captured by the English and Spanish during the Rough Wooing and 17 years later, Mary Queen of Scots, having returned from France, sought refuge here for a few days.

The castle was extended by the Regent Morton in 1574, and after James VI of Scotland reached his majority in 1579, he and his wife Anne of Denmark, often took up residence. It was at Dalkeith Castle that their first child Princess Margaret Stuart was born the following year, only to die two years later.

Their eldest son who succeeded his father as Charles I liked the estate so much that he contemplated purchasing it from the Earl of Morton to create a deer park. However, with the Wars of the Three Kingdoms, the transaction fell through and, in 1642, Dalkeith Castle was sold to Francis Scott, second Earl of Buccleuch whose only daughter Anne had married James, Duke of Monmouth, natural son of Charles II.

It proved an altogether traumatic union. Charles created her Duchess of Buccleuch in her own right and following her husband's execution for treason against his uncle James VII and II, she was allowed to retain her title and estates. After the Glorious Revolution, she approached the Scottish architect James Smith to remodel the house in the style of William of Orange's palace. A part of the old tower house of the old castle was installed in the new structure.

When the exiled Charles Stuart was proclaimed King of Scots in February 1649, General Monck, who had previously been a Royalist supporter, came north with Oliver Cromwell to fight, and be victorious, at the Battle of Dunbar. He was subsequently made Commander in Chief in Scotland and took up residence at Dalkeith between 1650 and 1652, then 1654 and 1659, planting an avenue of trees known today as Monck's Walk.

However, it was not until the 18th century that the full renovation was undertaken by William Walker and Benjamin Robinson, and the Montagu Bridge was built and designed by Robert Adam. Further changes were made by William Burn in the 19th century.

Among those who spent time at Dalkeith were Prince Charles Edward Stuart for two nights in 1746; George IV during his theatrical visit to Edinburgh in 1822 and Queen Victoria in 1842, preferring this countryside setting to the then grim streets surrounding Holyrood.

Lady Elizabeth Montagu was the eldest daughter of the Duke of Montagu and a great granddaughter of Charles Churchill, Duke of Marlborough. Under her patronage, and that of the third Duke, a cast of exceptional thinkers and performers of the Scottish Enlightenment period were welcomed to Dalkeith Palace, including the educational innovator Anne Young; star soprano Angelica Catalani; Scottish music advocates Niel and Nathaniel Gow; Ignatius Sancho, the first composer of African descent to publish his music in Britain; and Domenico Corri, his wife La Miniatrice and brother Natale Corri, who were central to musical life in Edinburgh in the late 18th and early 19th centuries. Surely this was a beacon for the Edinburgh Festival which emerged over a century later?

Since then Dalkeith Palace has only occasionally been used by the Buccleuch family, serving over the latter half of the 20th century as an outpost of the University of Wisconsin until 2021. Now under the Buccleuch Living Heritage Trust, in the hands of Walter, Lord Dalkeith, wonderful things have been happening to integrate the Palace and Country Park into the local community.

The Steekit Yetts

There is one property that truly embodies the spirit of Richard Demarco and the Edinburgh Festival, unlike any other, and that is Traquair House at Innerleithen in the Peeblesshire valley of the River Tweed.

The lands of Traquair were once part of a royal hunting forest and, over the centuries, Traquair House has played host to 27 kings on sporting excursions into the rich surroundings of Ettrick and Lauderdale. Long ago there were bears, wild cats, wolves and boars in large quantities to be found here. Although no written confirmation exists, it can be assumed that a dwelling of sorts existed long before Alexander I stayed here in 1107 and granted Traquair a Royal Charter.

In the 15th century, King James III gifted these lands to a number of his favourites but latterly to his half-brother the Earl of Buchan. Thereafter, they passed to Buchan's natural son James Stuart, ancestor of the present owner.

Located in the lush, rolling hills of Peeblesshire, the old fortress stands today a quarter of a mile from where the River Tweed winds its leisurely course from Peebles to the tiny town of Innerleithen.

Once that lovely water passed so close to the house that it was said the Laird could fish from his windows, but when the front of the house was remodelled, the course of the river was altered to avoid flooding.

Enlargements to the original keep had already begun when James Stuart of Traquair died fighting with his King against the English at the Battle of Flodden in 1513. In 1599, his grandson, Sir William Stuart, created the main house as it can be seen today, extending the existing building southwards and adding the steep slated roof and dormer windows. The low two-storey wings, ornamental wrought-iron gateway and screen which encloses the courtyard, date from the 17th century.

In 1633, Sir John Stuart, seventh Laird, was created Lord Stuart of Traquair, then first Earl of Traquair, by Charles I. Lord Traquair soon became Lord High Treasurer of Scotland, but his loyal support of his king was to lose him everything and he died in poverty in 1659.

The second Earl fought alongside his father in the civil wars, and both were taken prisoner at the Battle of Preston. The fourth and fifth earls followed in the tradition as dedicated Jacobites (supporters of the royal line of Stuart). The latter was imprisoned in the Tower of London for two years. A reminder of this time at Traquair is embodied in the 'bear' entrance gates, also known as the 'Steekit Yetts', which stand at the end of a tree-flanked avenue.

These gates were closed following a visit from Prince Charles Edward Stuart on an autumn day in 1745. It was pronounced that they would not be opened again until a Stuart is returned to the British throne, and they have not been opened since.

The seventh Earl who mostly lived abroad in Europe, was succeeded by his son who, leaving no male heir, passed the inheritance to his sister who died in 1875 aged 100.

Thereafter the estate passed to a cousin, Henry Constable-Maxwell of Terregles, a son of the tenth Lord Herries, and it was he who added the Stuart name to his own. From him, the inheritance passed to Peter Maxwell Stuart, 20th Laird, who continued to open the house to public with the support of his remarkable wife Flora. Together they transformed the care worn old family home into one of Scotland's most compelling visitor attractions, complete with its own fine ale brewery.

In her memoir, *A Gift of Time*, Flora recalls a couple of expeditions led by Richard Demarco. 'Richard lives in perpetual motion, travels from one country to another and is known to everyone in the art world, all over Europe,' she noted. 'He is interested in everyone he meets, boosts artists' confidence, tends to promise them the world and passes on. One of his friends has aptly described him as "an artwork in himself".'

The first time Flora accompanied Richard on an EDINBURGH ARTS expedition was with six or seven others when they went to the monastery of St Benedictusberg in The Netherlands. This modern church, designed by the Benedictine monk Hans van der Lann, was beautiful in its stark simplicity. As Flora followed Richard into the church, he observed that if these people had not been here, we would not exist. 'I had never heard the value of prayer described so succinctly,' she said.

On a visit to Hungary, Flora recalled that their group grew as various artists joined them from Romania and Serbia. 'At night we trailed after Richard through the streets of Budapest looking for a restaurant for dinner while he pointed out the details of the architecture and revelled in the beauty of the city. We became so many that no restaurant would take us in until an old haunt took pity on us and we finally sat down at a huge banqueting table where dinner was enlivened by a speech from a female Serbian trade union leader.'

During the Edinburgh Festival of 2008, the 17th century library of Traquair provided the venue for a two-day symposium on the Benedictine history of Scotland, as well as a forum for Polish–Scottish cultural dialogue; there had been earlier exhibitions in the grounds of Traquair House by Paul Neagu, Joanna Przybyla and Deryk Healey.

Flora was an invaluable early supporter of the Demarco band-wagon, a committed involvement that has been continued by her lively daughter and son-in-law, Catherine Maxwell Stuart and her husband Mark Muller Stuart KC. From its beginning in 2010, the annual Beyond Borders International Festival at the end of August has been a major fixture in the Demarco calendar. One of its core principles is the commitment to providing a platform for international dialogue, acknowledging that bringing people together from different countries, backgrounds or specialisms who may not ordinarily meet, allows them to learn about and from each other through sharing experience, the ideas and the challenges that they face in their own contexts.

Says Mark Muller Stuart, 'International dialogue allows independent communities of thinkers to come together in order to find new solutions to common problems and misunderstandings. The need of human beings to physically come face to face with each other to settle differences and think through solutions to common threats is as old as human history itself.'

9

Skateraw Barn, Arniston and Falkland

"LET US TAKE ONE PRACTICAL EXAMPLE OF THE TRUTH OF FAIRY TALES. IN THESE STORIES SUCCESS IS MADE TO DEPEND ON A NUMBER OF SMALL MATERIAL OBJECTS AND OBSERVANCES; LIFE IS A CHAIN OF TALISMANS. IF A MAN TOUCHES THREE TREES IN PASSING HE IS SAFE; IF HE TOUCHES FOUR, HE IS RUINED. IF THE HERO MEETS A MILLER HE IS TO ANSWER NONE OF HIS QUESTIONS. IF HE PLUCKS A RED FLOWER IN A PARTICULAR MEADOW, HE WILL HAVE POWER OVER THE MIGHTY KINGS OF SOME DISTANT CITY. NOW THIS POETIC SENSE OF THE DECISIVENESS OF SOME FLYING DETAIL IS A THOUSAND TIMES MORE GENUINE AND PRACTICAL THAN THE POMPOUS INSISTENCE ON SOME MORAL OR SCIENTIFIC LAW"

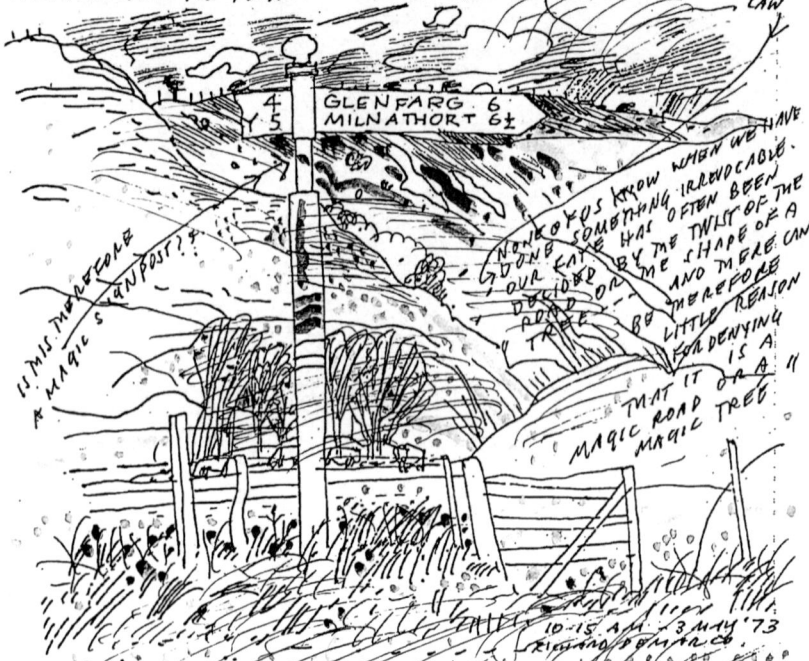

IS THIS THEREFORE A MAGIC SIGNPOST??

GLENFARG 6
MILNATHORT 6½
4 5

NONE OF US KNOW WHEN WE HAVE DONE SOMETHING IRREVOCABLE OUR FATE HAS OFTEN BEEN DECIDED BY THE TWIST OF THE ROAD OR THE SHAPE OF A TREE AND THERE CAN BE THEREFORE LITTLE REASON FOR DENYING THAT IT IS A MAGIC ROAD OR A MAGIC TREE

OF COURSE "THE ROAD TO MEIKLE SEGGIE" IS A SMALL PART OF A NETWORK OF ANCIENT TRACKS, AS DROVERS ROAD ON WHICH FARMERS AND SHEPHERDS WALKED THEIR ANIMALS — THEIR CATTLE & SHEEP TO MARKET. MY ITALIAN ANCESTORS WERE SHEPHERDS

10-15 AM 3 MAY '73
RICHARD DEMARCO

AT THE PASS OF CONDIE (ALSO CALLED PATHSTRUIE) WHERE THE MAY WATER FLOWS UNDER A 300-YEAR OLD STONE BRIDGE, BESIDE TWO OLD CROFTS, THERE IS AN OLD METAL ROAD SIGN WITH ONE OF ITS ARMS BADLY BROKEN SO THAT IN MAKING THE DECISION TO TURN LEFT YOU CONTINUE IN THE SPIRIT OF ADVENTURE AND WITH FULL RESPECT FOR THE MYSTERY OF THE ROAD TO MEIKLE SEGGIE YOU HAVE TO FORSAKE THE KNOWN FOR THE UNKNOWN, FOR THE REASSURING FACT THAT MILNATHORT IS 6½ MILES DISTANT FOR THE UNCERTAINTY THAT 5 MILES DISTANT IS A DESTINATION DEFINED BY THE LETTER "Y"

Skateraw

THE SMALL SETTLEMENT of Skateraw, now a farm, was formerly the site of a World War One military aerodrome on East Lothian's North Sea coast. Today, the land sits ominously close to the Torness Nuclear Power Station. Coupled with the rich laterite soil, there are also rich lime deposits which have been exploited for centuries, most recently by the nearby Tarmac Lafarge Cement Works at Whitesands.

In 1787, Scotland's bard Robert Burns much admired this vista as he passed this way with his lawyer friend Robert Ainslie on a visit to the nearby town of Dunbar. From February 2005 until 2009, with funding from Creative Scotland and Dunbar's Museum dedicated to the boyhood of the environmentalist John Muir, the Demarco Collection was housed in a vast grain store barn generously provided by the farmer Johnny Watson. On display, along with his personal archive, were 10,000 works from 50 countries and a vast wall of black-and-white photographs recording his many exploits on The Road to Meikle Seggie.

Johnny and his wife Sandra arrived at Skateraw several years after her father Jack W Taylor had bought the farm from the Bowes family. The Taylor family were from Falkirk where their agricultural enterprise had been overrun and consumed by a massive British Petroleum development. So they moved on.

At Skateraw, the climate was ideal for the growing of wheat for distilling and bread and biscuit making, barley for malting and soups, Brussels sprouts destined for supermarkets and potatoes to meet the escalating demand for chips. In fact, the best of everything.

Johnny is the third generation of a family of West Linton-based seed merchants and eventually bought the farm over from his father-in-law. Deeply aware of the spiritual quality of this landscape's alluring and pastoral beauty, he instantly connected the extremes of coastal beauty and rich abundance of wildlife caught between the stark icons of the modern world – 'Linking urban and rural living through the media of art and agriculture.' Writing for Demarco 2020, Johnny wrote:

> I first remember driving Richard over the fields around Torness, next door to Skateraw, fields that I have farmed for many years as a tenant. I had always thought that the enormous blank wall

of the power station, facing the farm, would make a great site to project some images on, or maybe a film.

We both wanted to further link the Archive in the barn with the surrounding environment, both the farm and, of course, the nuclear power station. We wanted to give visitors a better idea of Richard's belief that art and science are inter-related in response perhaps to his favourite artist – Leonardo da Vinci – the supreme artist-scientist. With generous financial support from British Energy, we commissioned the film-maker Ken McMullen to present his work *Lumine de Lumine* (*Light out of Light*) which was viewed by over 500 guests and received critical acclaim from not only the press but also through the BBC *Culture Show* with Charles Hazelwood.

For four years, Skateraw Barn provided the Demarco Archive with an inspirational platform to advance its presence and existence in a rural setting and reach a new generation of appreciative audiences. Masterclasses were introduced for East Lothian and Berwickshire schoolchildren. Outstanding among these was the Chess Match supervised by international chess master Craig Pritchett involving Dunbar Primary School Children, a replay of the historic match played by Marcel Duchamp and a group of Dutch students.

Under the direction of Professor Elizabeth Ogilvie, her students at Edinburgh College of Art and Architecture presented two excellent exhibitions taking careful account of both the landscape and seascape at Skateraw. Leading figures from the international art world commented that a visit to the Skateraw project left them convinced that the Demarco Archive represented the spirit of the Scottish Enlightenment in deference to luminaries such as John Muir, James Hutton, David Hume, Lord Kames and Robert Burns, each of whom hold a historic connection to Skateraw and its surroundings.

The Arniston estate

The Dundas family, with their original 15th-century family seat of Dundas Castle at South Queensferry, acquired the Arniston estate 11 miles south of Edinburgh in 1571 for James Dundas, the youngest son by the second marriage of the 16th Laird of Dundas. An open courtyard was built for him, probably on the foundations of an original tower house which is thought to have belonged to the Knights of St John. From this base, James fathered one of the most dazzling Presbyterian legal dynasties with five successive generations represented on the Supreme Court of Scotland, each taking the judicial title of Lord Arniston.

It was not until 1688 that the second Lord Arniston set about making further improvements to his home, although 37 years were to pass before he engaged the architect William Adam to build him a splendid new residence. He had left it a bit late as he died the following year but his son Robert, the next Lord Arniston, who during his father's lifetime had risen to become Solicitor General for Scotland, then Lord Advocate, was equally committed.

As with a number of his projects, William Adam made the best of what had been there before. A section of the old house is incorporated into the main hall while the 17th century Oak Room at the back remains virtually intact. However, it is the details of Adam's spectacular interiors which remain a triumph, especially the hall with its spectacular plasterwork by the brilliant Dutch stuccoist Joseph Enzer whom Adam also employed for two other Scottish projects – Yester House in East Lothian and the House of Dun, near Brechin.

Unashamedly Classical, Baroque and Rococo styles are blended to create a breathtaking impact. Upstairs in the former library, transformed during the 19th century into the Porcelain Room, the plasterwork is equally dramatic.

All would have gone well had it not been for the expense of creating the elaborate formal garden. There was a waterfall over white stone on the hill beyond the house which by means of a mechanical device could be turned on and off, an amazing extravagance at the time. At this stage the budget started to get out of hand and Lord Arniston, with a family of nine children to bring up and educate, pulled the plug on further expenditure.

His son and heir, the fourth Lord Arniston, inherited a massive mountain of debt but had happily married Henrietta Carmichael, a substantial heiress, whose inheritance proved critical to the completion of the house. The chosen architect this time was William Adam's son John, who amended his father's plans and instructed for rooms to be built on two floors instead of three, while maintaining the original facade.

To say that the fourth Lord Arniston was a bit of a collector is a massive understatement. The set of terracotta portrait busts which look down on the Porcelain Room were acquired when he was at Utrecht University and took the opportunity to explore Italy. In the same room are displays of Meissen, Sevres sets and Beilby glass.

The ancestral portraits date back to the 16th century with fine examples of the work of Sir Henry Raeburn and Allan Ramsay. Among them is a portrait of Henry Dundas, Viscount Melville, half-brother of the fourth Lord Arniston who was War Minister and Home Secretary in William Pitt the Younger's government, and for his overlord status in Scottish Politics earned the sobriquet of The Uncrowned King of Scotland.

As had by then almost become a family tradition, Robert Dundas, son of the fourth Lord Arniston, in turn rose to the Supreme Court as the fifth Lord Arniston, although he declined to become President of the Court of Session for health reasons. To compensate, he plunged his energies into improving his estate which he extensively furnished with gateways and bridges fabricated in stonework which he acquired from the facade of Old Parliament House in Edinburgh when it was demolished around 1808.

Further improvements were made to the great house in the 19th century; a porch on the north side was added and the colonnades linking the pavilions were heightened. The stone floor of the hall was replaced by parquet.

When at the age of 30 Althea Dundas inherited Arniston House in 1971 from her Aunt May, she said the prospect of keeping it wind and watertight seemed almost overwhelming. An outbreak of dry rot during the 1950s had led to John Adam's rooms being stripped of timber and internal plasterwork. In 1980, the roof of the main block had to be entirely removed.

Fortunately, she is a resourceful lady and was wholeheartedly supported by her able South African husband Aedrian Dundas-Bekker until his untimely death in 1990. With financial support from Historic Scotland, the national conservation agency, the necessary repair work was eventually completed. More recently, the management of the 40-room mansion has been taken over by Aedrian and Althea's capable daughter Henrietta.

The ultimate royal retreat

On a visit to Falkland Palace in 2024, Marek Mutor, Deputy Director of the Ossoliński National Institute of Poland, based in Wrocław, was astonished to come across a posthumous painting of Mary Queen of Scots dressed by an unknown artist, almost identical to the one on display at the Ossoliński Institute. How amazing it is that the two great collections of Europe should share such a poignant a link with the House of Stuart.

The Royal House of Stewart took possession of the Falkland estate and its earldom in 1371 when the last MacDuff Countess of Fife (no relation to the 21st century folk band!) made it over to her brother-in-law Robert Stewart, Duke of Albany, brother of Robert III.

In 1402, David, Duke of Rothesay, heir to Robert III, died unpleasantly while staying with his uncle, who when his other nephew James was taken prisoner in England, took up the role of Governor of Scotland. It was generally believed that Albany had contrived David's death in order to place his own son on the Scottish throne, added to which he made no effort to liberate his nephew.

However, once James was released to return to Scotland as James I in 1424, both Albany and his son were executed for treason and their possessions, including Falkland Castle in the Kingdom of Fife, passed to the Crown as a much-loved holiday retreat. In 1451, James II built on an extension and eight years later gifted the castle to his queen, Mary of Gueldres. Seven years later the small town that had sprung up on the estate was given Royal Burgh status and the castle became a palace.

James III spent much of his childhood here but it was his son James IV who took a close interest in improving the facilities and built the south range of the complex.

The style was very much of its time, rudimentary Gothic, but then along came James V. Having recently returned from a visit to the French Court in 1537, he had seen just how successfully Italian Renaissance style could be blended with French castellated Gothic.

James' architect, Sir James Hamilton of Finnart, was instructed with the understanding that all of the craftsmen employed should either be French or French-trained. The result is the exquisite Renaissance ornament on the courtyard of the south range.

It should be understood, however, that Falkland essentially served only as a country retreat for the Stewarts, used primarily for the practice of falconry and hunting of deer and wild boar in the forests of Fife. Away from Dunfermline, Linlithgow and Holyrood, it was remote from Court life and place of escape. Thus it was that James v, already ill from his defeat at the battle of Solway Moss, chose to die here a week after his daughter, the future Mary Queen of Scots was born. Note that the Stewart surname was changed to Stuart following Mary's accession to the Scottish throne.

Falkland Palace still belongs to the Crown. However, as was the custom with Royal castles, it was officially placed in the safekeeping of a hereditary keeper, often a relative of the monarch. In this case, it was granted to a scion of the Crichton-Stuart family descended from a natural son of Robert II whose descendants eventually rose through the ranks to become Marquesses of Bute.

The responsibility for the palace passed to the current branch of this family in 1887. However, 55 years later, following consultation with HM The Queen, Major Michael Crichton-Stuart, son of the third Marquess of Bute, appointed the National Trust for Scotland as Deputy Keeper. In addition, he provided a financial endowment for the palace's future upkeep.

His son Ninian Crichton-Stuart, a dedicated conservationist, inherited the role of Hereditary Keeper in 1991. A characterful individual, he describes his position as an 'anomaly of history' and admits to being deeply ambivalent about privilege. 'I ran away from home in my late teens to find myself through living and working with homeless people in Glasgow,' he confesses.

All this is a far cry from his current surroundings. From the entrance hall of the gatehouse you ascend into the Keeper's suite on the second floor where the bedroom is dominated by James VI's magnificent canopied bed. The room is hung with copies of full-length Royal portraits. The drawing room was restored by the third Marquess of Bute in the 1890s. On the oak ceiling are the coats-of-arms of the Stuart kings, and those of the different keepers of the palace. Of course, portraits include Mary Queen of Scots, Charles II and Catherine of Braganza.

Outstanding features in the 16th century interior of the Royal Chapel are the oak screen between chapel and ante-chapel, and the

painted ceiling which was specially decorated for the visit of Charles
I in 1633. The tapestry gallery is hung with 17th century Flemish
tapestries and furnished with replicas of 16th and 17th century pieces
of furniture. The old library displays memorabilia from the 20th
century belonging to the Crichton-Stuarts.

Of specific interest at Falkland are the Royal tennis courts, built
in 1539 prior to Henry VIII's Court at Hampton Court in England.
'Royal' or 'Real' tennis differs from that played, for example, at
Wimbledon. For a start, Kings had their servants hit the first ball to
begin a game, hence the expression 'serve'.

In 1965, a 'Real Tennis' Club was formed at Falkland by local
enthusiasts. The 'Real' tennis racquet was invented in Italy in 1583,
44 years after the Royal Court in Scotland was built. It is smaller
than the conventional racquet in that its head is the shape of a palm,
given that the game was originally played with the hand. In 1989, the
450th anniversary of the Falkland Court's creation was marked by
an international tournament won by the Falkland Palace Club and
attended by Prince Edward, now Duke of Edinburgh.

Falkland Palace was, of course, a nodal point on a number of
Richard Demarco's EDINBURGH ARTS expeditions on The Road
to Meikle Seggie.

10

Mellerstain and Marchmont

AMONG THE PARTICIPANTS JANE HAD TO CONSIDER WERE BRENDA'S SNÆBJÖRNSDOTTIR - PATRICIA DOLNWA... - ROSE FRAIN - CLARE TRACKER (who was directing EDINBURGH ARTS performances involving her fellow PARTICIPANTS) ANNE SEAGRAVE was also a performance ARTIST who was making "SOLO" performances EXPERIENCED EDINBURGH ARTERS" WORD NANCE... move to help Terry Newman and Sally DUNMORE. JANE CHISHOLM and ANNE GORING

THANKFULLY THE PROGRAMMING in WROCLAW was in the capable hands of OLA AND TOMOT) FALENDER — THE POLISH ARTISTS ZBIGNIEN MAKAROWICZ BARBARA KOSCOWSKA WHO WERE ALSO DIRECTING GALLERY "X" ZBIGNIEN WAS ALSO THE PRESIDENT OF THE Polish UNION OF ARTISTS

THERE WERE 33 PARTICIPANTS IN ALL.

JANE McALLISTER in contemplative mood enjoying A MOMENT OF PEACE AFTER dinner in WROCLAW whilst on the 1990 EDINBURGH ARTS expedition to POLAND. As usual on these expeditions she had the invaluable task of dealing with the daily programme AND THE needs of the ARTISTS we were MEETING — TEN YEARS OF EDINBURGH ARTS "TRAVELS HAD MADE HER INVALUABLE AS THE "ARTIST AS EXPLORER".

Extra-terrestial messages

MELLERSTAIN HOUSE, NEAR Gordon, in Berwickshire, is widely recognised as the finest surviving example of the work of the great Scottish architect Robert Adam. It contains the best of his decorated ceilings in their original mauve, green and terracotta colours from the 18th century.

Mellerstain remains the magnificent home of the earls of Haddington, and has been since their ancestor George Baillie of Jerviswood, the son of a flourishing Lanarkshire merchant, acquired the estate in 1642.

Through marriage and patronage, the property was passed on to two earls of Haddington who in 1725 employed first William Adam to build the two wings, then his son Robert to design the central block and subsequently supervise the magnificent interior decoration.

The 17th-century heroine of Mellerstain has to be Grizel Hume, daughter of Sir Patrick Hume, later first Earl of Marchmont. Aged 12, she was called upon to visit her father's friend and fellow Covenanter George Baillie, who had been imprisoned in the Tolbooth of Edinburgh accused of treason. With her, the little girl carried a letter from her father which would have caused an outrage had it been discovered.

For their Covenanting sympathies, the Humes were exiled from Scotland to Holland, where Grizel, somewhat older, was courted by George's son, another George, penniless after his father's execution in 1684. However, when William of Orange took over the British throne in 1689, the situation changed overnight. Large numbers of confiscated estates were restored to their original owners and Grizel Hume married George to become Grizel Baillie. Their youngest daughter Rachel married Charles, Lord Binning in 1771 and their eldest son succeeded his grandfather as seventh Earl of Haddington. Their youngest son took the name Baillie when he inherited the Mellerstain estate and in a later generation, his son inherited both the earldom and the estate.

The interiors and outward appearance of the great house has changed little over the past three and a half centuries. However, the spectacular south-facing terrace and loggia were added in 1909 by Sir Reginald Blomfield, who also enlarged the lake. There is so much to see and admire. The bold plaques along the tops of the bookcases in the library show Roman and other antique scenes. The collection of books, mostly collected in the 18th century by George Baillie bear his bookplate of 1724 as one of the Lords of Treasury. Six marble busts are set in recesses above the library doors.

Of particular beauty is the ceiling in the music room which is decorated with sphinxes and eagles. This is a house of great European distinction.

It was when Joseph Beuys accepted an invitation from Tadusz Kantor to participate in a performance of the Cricot Two Theatre production of the Witkiewicz play *Lovelies and Dowdies* at the Forrest Hill Poorhouse, that Lord (John) Binning, later to succeed his father in 1966 as 13th Earl of Haddington, came into the sphere of the Demarco Gallery. In June 1983, an installation of sculpture by Denise Marika was transferred from the Demarco Gallery in Jeffrey Street to Mellerstain to great critical acclaim.

The exhibition was focused on the increasing numbers of refugees fleeing from world conflicts, a crisis as thought-provoking then as it is now.

A noted photographer, John, known as 'Binning' to his close friends, was throughout his life fascinated by the phenomena of crop circles, notably the one that fleetingly appeared at Whitsome on a former burial ground of Cistercian monks. Although considered by some to be a trifle eccentric, he seriously believed that they were a form of extra-terrestrial messaging from beyond. Around this time, he became a sponsor of *The Cereologist* magazine which was devoted to the topic. A popular figure in social circles, his other passions included ballooning and beekeeping which involved him annually taking his bees up into the Lammermuirs to enjoy the heather.

Embracing a dream

The pavilion wings of this magnificent Grade 'A' listed Palladian mansion embrace the long front drive from the north-east. One of Berwickshire's greatest architectural triumphs. Marchmont House at Greenlaw was begun in 1750 to enhance the status of Hugh Hume-Campbell, Lord Polwarth, who succeeded to the Peerage as third Earl of Marchmont, and who in 1763 became Governor of the Bank of Scotland and was keeper of the Great Seal of Scotland until his death in 1794.

Influences of William Adam and James Gibb are recognisable but the consensus is that this was largely the work of the lesser known architect Thomas Gibson from Edinburgh, who took up where the others left off. Most striking of all from its early beginnings are the two principal interiors of the saloon and drawing room, both featuring spectacular George II period plasterwork by the leading 18th century plasterer Thomas Clayton.

Hugh Hume-Campbell inherited his earldom from his father who had added the surname of Campbell on his marriage to Margaret, heiress to the wealthy Sir George Campbell of Cessnock in Ayrshire. Descended from the poet and courtier Sir Patrick Hume of Polwarth and Redbraes, Hugh's grandfather, a staunch Covenanter, was forced into exile overseas before taking part in William of Orange's Glorious Revolution of 1688. With his estates restored to him, he was created Earl of Marchmont in 1697.

Like so many of Scotland's great houses, Marchmont House simply evolved. Alterations were made to the rear elevation in the mid-19th century by William Burn. However, it was only after the estate was sold to Robert Finnie McEwen in the early 20th century that the building we see today came into its true splendour. By lowering the ground floor at the front of the house, the Edinburgh-based architect Sir Robert Lorimer transformed the entrance with the addition of a porch and added a top floor with dormer windows. In addition, he connected the pavilions on either side internally.

A two-storey open internal hall surmounted by an oval cupola was introduced, and the main staircase was replaced by a grander staircase on the right-hand side. The dining room and library were moved around, and a magnificent double storey oak-panelled music room was created.

Dominating this music room is an imposing organ with 1,962 pipes supplied by WE Hill & Son and Norman & Beard of Norwich (the two firms merged during the installation) and implemented by Sir Robert Lorimer in 1919. A lawyer by profession, Robert Finnie McEwen was himself an accomplished musician and set several songs by Robert Burns and Sir Walter Scott to music. His son John, a Scottish unionist politician who served under Winston Churchill as Lord of Treasury during the Second World War, was rewarded with a baronetcy in 1953.

The Demarco Gallery's association with Marchmont began through

Richard's close friendship with the dazzling, self-trained artist Rory McEwen. Countless conversations on the nature of modern art ensued. It was at Rory's insistence that the Board of the Demarco Gallery was strengthened with the addition of his younger brother John Sebastian and his elder brother Robin who in the 1970s became Chairman.

As great-grandchildren of Robert Finnie McEwen, the brothers were all immensely talented musicians, artists and writers. During the 1960s, Rory and Alex formed a folk band in addition to the former establishing a reputation as an accomplished botanical artist. It was their equally talented elder brother, Sir Robin, third Baronet, who illustrated the naturalist and otter keeper Gavin Maxwell's bestselling books *Ring of Bright Water* and *The Rocks Remain*.

The 1960s was a golden age for Scottish folk music with Rory playing a 12-string guitar, paving the way for perhaps the better-remembered Robin Hall and Jimmie Macgregor and, of course, The Corries. Billy Connolly, Van Morrison and Eric Burdon of The Animals have all acknowledged Rory's influence on their careers.

Multi-talented, impeccably good looking and so well connected as to run with the Princess Margaret set, the future of the brothers in show business seemed assured. Bob Dylan, John Lennon, the Everly Brothers and the Indian composer and sitarist Ravi Shankar were among those who frequented Rory's London home.

Of course, nothing lasts forever. The following year the brothers decided to split up from their singing duo, with Alex joining the newspaper and magazine distributor John Menzies while Rory pursued his true passion as sculptor and painter. Aside from his brilliant botanic illustrations, Rory embarked upon a wide range of different media. After the mercurial Richard Demarco lured the German performance artist Joseph Beuys to Edinburgh and introduced him to Rory, three lifelong friendships were forged.

The collaboration between Joseph Beuys and Richard Demarco is the stuff of legend but not so very much is known of their mutual interaction with Rory led to a documentary film shot on Rannoch Moor.

When Rory abandoned his music career for art, the *Scotsman* art critic Edward Gage wrote of him, 'We have seen him turn from the life of a troubadour... and embark on a series of experiments that have quickly led him beyond the frontiers of painting, to sculpture and, most recently, to the concept of the environment.'

'Rory's saturated tiny paintings resonate with an astonishing depth of life and colour,' observed his daughter Sam, herself now an acclaimed artist on the New York scene. 'People who own his work don't want to sell them.'

Rory died in 1982 and following the death of his elder brother Sir Robin, the Marchmont estates were sold in 1988. The farms were bought by Oliver Burge, a successful London-based businessman. For the following 20 years, the great house, stripped of its contents at an auction, served as a Sue Ryder Nursing Home.

When the nursing home closed in 2005, Marchmont House once again came onto the market and Oliver Burge's engaging and gifted son Hugo, who had by then created his own successful IT business empire, stepped into the breach to fulfil a childhood dream. It was Hugo's greatest ambition to create a hub for makers and creators within the outbuildings of Marchmont, backed up as an international venue for conferences and seminar events. His achievement over a short period of substantial restoration work was breathtaking.

Upon the roof, he symbolically placed an Antony Gormley statue gazing south towards the Cheviots, a metaphor for all that is great about the outward-looking and visionary spirit underlined through the centuries by the occupants of Marchmont House, past and present.

To attend The Spirit of Rory McEwen tribute, hosted by Hugo at the end of April 2022, was to step back into a world of free-spirited creativity and flamboyant eccentricity, underscored by those who attended. Family and friends, all contributed highly individual reminiscences, not least Rory's four children Sam, Flora, Christabel and Adam who were accompanied by a veritable army of siblings. A special Artist Residency space was introduced in Fogo Cottage at Marchmont, Rory's former print studio.

'Rory McEwen literally changed my life,' said the English interior designer Nicholas Haslam who first met Rory while staying with the Astors at Cliveden. For years he and Rory had occupied studios in London next to one another.

'Rory had a great capacity for friendship,' recalled his cousin Lord Hesketh who spent much of his childhood at Marchmont. 'At Marchmont there is no outside noise,' he explained. 'It provides the perfect environment for musicians, poets and artists.'

'Our family has always loved being in Berwickshire,' Hugo told

Roddy Martine in 2016. 'When Marchmont House came up for sale in 2005, Marchmont Farms Ltd – after much hesitation and some consternation – exercised our right of pre-emption and bought it. It made so much sense to put the house and land back together rather than let them be split onto uncertain journeys.'

Marchmont was an unexpected life development for him and on a scale that he would never have dreamed of, or conceived. It faced him with a daunting sense of duty and responsibility but at the same time provided him with the opportunity he had always wanted to celebrate creativity. It was, he admitted, an incredible canvas to work on.

Hugo's secret ambition growing up, he told Roddy Martine, was to perhaps become an artist or designer of some sort, 'with a soft spot for wood craftsmanship and sculpture.'

Instead, he had embarked upon a dizzying entrepreneurial IT journey creating Cheapflights and co-founding HOWZAT Partners in 2006. Ultimately, his Momondo Group was acquired by Booking Group in 2016 as US leader in the sector. Such was the serendipity that led him to become the saviour of Marchmont House.

It was a challenge willingly taken on by Hugo and his father Oliver – fellow Directors of Marchmont Farms Limited – in a huge team effort. A six-year restoration project was launched to create a sensitive, appropriate atmosphere in the house, and to celebrate artistic endeavour and to focus on the Arts & Crafts movement in the later Lorimer areas.

With the overall project management overseen by Hugh Garratt of Smith & Garratt, Chartered Surveyors of nearby Ladykirk, a determined effort was made to employ local craftsmen. In the event, over 80 per cent of the work was carried out by local trades.

The house also needed to replenish its contents and to budget for the acquisition of fine period furniture and rugs, not to mention a breathtaking picture collection which today features splendid portraits by Sir Henry Raeburn, Allan Ramsay, Alexander Nasmyth and John Scougal. Paintings from the early 20th century include Samuel Peploe, Francis Cadell and JD Fergusson.

With so much energy and innovation, it came as no surprise that in 2016, Marchmont House was given a special award for Conservation and Design in the Scottish Borders Design Awards. In 2017, it attracted the Georgian Group Award and, in 2018, won the coveted Historic

Houses and Sotheby's Restoration of the Year Award for the United Kingdom.

Hugo admitted he enjoyed living life vicariously through the creativity of others. His enthusiasm and generosity were infectious. He relished being in a position to bring together the works of modernist sculptors such as Barbara Hepworth, Henry Moore, Lynn Chadwick, Eduardo Paolozzi, Gerald Laing, William Turnbull and, more recently, Stephen Cox, in addition to commissioning local artists Frippy Jameson, Charlie Poulsen and Keith McCarter. A solitary figure by Antony Gormley stands on the roof.

'I like to think people feel good about coming here,' he said. 'The Scottish Borders is such a wonderful location for creativity. The more I look around, the more I find.'

And he was discernibly excited to establish The Marchmont Workshop to accommodate apprentices who had been training with Lawrence Neal at his workshop in Stockton, Warwickshire. Thus was created a lineage stretching back to furniture makers Ernest Gimson, James Maclaren and Philip Clissett. In April 2020, these apprentices stepped up to manage the ongoing business and become the last craftspeople in Britain to make rush seat chairs for a living.

Six other artists' units were opened around communal areas to mark a new chapter for the arts and to celebrate creativity in the Scottish Borders.

Hugo's mission statement was that creativity needs to be imbued in the everyday life of the estate, 'Keeping the rich DNA of Marchmont alive for another generation.'

Not everyone has the opportunity to fulfil and more importantly, sustain their dream. It seemed that at Marchmont House, Hugo Burge was well on his way.

But in 2023, tragedy struck. In an unexplained accident, Hugo died at the age of 50. It is a loss that for those who knew him, albeit only briefly, find beyond comprehension. Mercifully, his vision lives on with the Marchmont Makar's Foundation he created, renamed the Hugo Burge Foundation and headed up by Executive Director Lucy Brown and Dr James Fox.

In the grounds of Marchmont House, Hugo commissioned a statue of a Girl with Acorn from the sculptress Frippy Jameson. He saw the acorn as a symbol for new ideas that would seed something meaningful. Mighty Oaks from Little Acorns Grow. God bless him. As Richard Demarco remarked in his filmed tribute, 'There will never be another Hugo Aylesford Burge.'

DunsPlayFest

Under the steerage of Sir John McEwen, son of Sir Robin, the DunsPlayFest was established in 2019 with funding from Creative Scotland as a nine-day long celebration of brand-new theatre and dramatic writing with performances and workshops taking place in the Duns Volunteer Hall in Berwickshire, known as Heart For Duns. With trustees Lucy Vaughan, Genny Dixon, Jerry Ponder, Michael Bevan, Ramsay Jones, Eric Branse-Instone, Karen Thomas and Jonathan Findlay, and producer Sara Best, Richard Demarco was invited to become patron. Featuring more than 60 performances – play premiers, rehearsed readings, workshops, cabaret acts, community events and several parties – the festival has grown attracting audiences from far and wide.

Sir John recalled that as a child he often heard Ricky's name mentioned, generally accompanied by something like astonishment. 'My father and two uncles served on one of his boards and things got a wee bit hairy sometimes; but you could tell there was much love,' he said.

Having been away from the theatre and the Scottish Borders for years, Sir John returned at length to both and (in 2013) invited Richard and Terry Ann Newman to a performance of *Glengarry Glen Ross* in which he played Richard Roma. 'To my delight they came all the way to Duns and were wonderfully encouraging. Then there was a show I wrote about Scotland and again they travelled the distance. He doesn't just talk the talk.

'But he does, indeed, talk. We could listen – my family and friends as astonished and as inspired as ever – for hours!'

When the DunsPlayFest festival of new drama was launched in 2019, Richard was the obvious choice as Patron. As co-founder of The Traverse, he was already a patron saint of new drama in Scotland and he has proved the perfect patron, a bubbling spring of encouragement and bonhomie.

'We are, of course, particularly pleased when he tells the audience that in DunsPlayFest the true spirit of the Edinburgh Festival lives on…!

'In 2022, when my Uncle Rory was being celebrated at Marchmont on the opening night of DunsPlayFest, Ricky was due to attend both occasions. As he left the house, the lift got stuck between floors and for some time there was panic and alarm.

'And in Duns we had to wait. Eventually the problem was solved and our hero arrived to make a sparkling and gracious speech.

'What a superstar he is, what a mighty brain he has, what an artist! How blessed we all feel to have ever known such a fellow.'

11

Tyde what may betide

IN 1917 PIET MONDRIAN SAW VISUAL REALITY AS AN ABSTRACTION OF LOOSE PARTICLES BLACK CROSSES AND STRIPES ON A WHITE CANVAS
IN 1961 ROBERT FILLIOU, THE FRENCH AVANT-GARDIST STATED "ARTISTIC ACTIVITY IS FOR ME A SPIRITUAL ACTIVITY"

PAUL VAN VLISSINGEN AND CAROLINE TISDALL INVITED ME TO A 5-DAY CONFERENCE INSPIRED BY THE LIFE AND WORK OF JOSEPH BEUYS

IT HELPED ME TO ACCEPT THE CHALLENGE OF GIVING "THE ADAM SMITH LECTURE THIS YEAR ON THE THEME USING THE WORDS OF BEUYS.

PIET MONDRIAN COMPOSITION IN BLACK AND WHITE (1917)

DETAIL OF ROBERT RAUSCHENBERG'S BIG D BILBAO 1990

"FRONT COVER OF THE BOOK ART MEETS SCIENCE AND SPIRITUALITY IN A CHANGING ECONOMY RECORDING A CONFERENCE AT THE STEDELIJK MUSEUM AMSTERDAM — 1990"

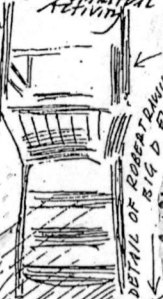

ART MEETS SCIENCE AND SPIRITUALITY

IN COLLABORATION WITH CAROLINE TISDALL AND PAUL FENTENER VAN VLISSINGEN LOUWRIEN WIJERS WAS ABLE TO DIRECT THIS HISTORIC EVENT

IN A CHANGING ECONOMY

"KUNST = KAPITAL" — OR OUR TRUE CAPITAL IS OUR CREATIVITY ROBERT RAUSCHENBERG STATED — THERE IS NO REASON NOT TO SEE THE ENTIRE WORLD AS A GIANT PAINTING

JOSEPH BEUYS 24 STUNDEN AT THE GALLERY PARNASS WUPPERTAL 1965

HIS HOLINESS THE 14TH DALAI LAMA OF TIBET MEETING WITH JOSEPH BEUYS IN BONN 27 OCTOBER 1982

THE PROTEST AGAINST PLACING MATTER ABOVE HUMAN VALUES AS CONCEIVED BY REMBRANDT WAS COMPLETED BY JOSEPH BEUYS
LOUWRIEN WIJERS IN HER FOREWORD ENTITLED "FROM A COMPETITIVE SOCIETY TO A COMPASSIONATE SOCIETY" REMINDED US THAT JOSEPH BEUYS DISTINGUISHED THREE LARGE CULTURAL SECTORS: THE ARTS, THE SCIENCES AND RELIGIOUS ACTIVITY —

THE DALAI LAMA LAUGHED HEARTILY AT JOSEPH BEUYS' REMARK THAT POLITICS SHOULD BE TURNED INTO ART HE REPLIED "VERY GOOD" WE ARE LACKING REAL LOVE AND FEELING, A SENSE OF BROTHERHOOD AND SISTERHOOD WE ARE NOT LACKING IN TECHNOLOGY OR SCIENCE, AN ARTIST CAN EXPRESS REAL HUMAN FEELINGS

Bemersyde

THROUGHOUT HISTORY WARTIME military heroes have thrown long shadows. When you are born into an ancient Scotch Whisky dynasty with a revered celebrity of a father aged 56, and you inherit his title and reputation when you are ten years old, there is a lot to come to live up to.

Sir Robin Philipson, President of the Royal Scottish Academy, a post he held from 1972 to 1983, once remarked to Roddy Martine that if George (generally known as Dawyck), second Earl Haig had not been the heir to an earldom, he would rightfully be recognised as one of the most significant Scottish painters of his generation.

Well, nothing is ever too late, but sadly Dawyck Haig who died in 2009, is no longer around to enjoy the accolade.

'Tyde what may betide, Haig shall be Haig of Bemersyde.' The 13th-century prophecy of Thomas the Rhymer certainly held fast. When in 1921, the future of the 14th-century Bemersyde tower house and estate, home to the Haig family at Melrose for over 800 years, looked uncertain, they were purchased from a Haig cousin by a Grateful Nation for Dawyck's father, ennobling him with an earldom and enabling him to become the 30th Laird of Bemersyde.

Does anyone nowadays remember the advertising slogan 'Don't be Vague. Ask for Haig' ? A fortuitous marriage in the 18th century between Kane Mackenzie Haig to Margaret Stein, whose father patented the continuous fuel efficient Coffey Still, led to Scotland's largest distillery at Clackmannan and those world-famous dimple three sided bottles.

Field Marshall Sir Douglas Haig was only able to enjoy his gift from a Grateful Nation for seven years before his death in 1928. For his son, however, Bemersyde, with the surrounding landscape steeped in the narrative of Sir Walter Scott, was the backdrop to his childhood and the muse for his art.

From Stowe School, Dawyck joined the Royal Scots Greys at the outbreak of the Second World War and was captured and imprisoned by the Germans in 1942. At Colditz Castle in Saxony, he joined a group of prisoners-of-war held hostage for their social connections and known as the 'Prominente'. Under lock and key, he recalled that it was his ability to draw and paint that kept his sanity.

When Colditz was liberated by the Americans in 1945, the other Prominente were liberated, but Haig was unwell and obliged to remain behind under guard at Königstein Castle on the River Elbe until finally freed by the Russians.

On release, he determined to make painting his career and he enrolled at Camberwell School of Arts in London before reclaiming Bemersyde and re-adapting himself to the life of a country laird in the Scottish Borders. Much of his time thereafter was defending the career and reputation of his father against the inevitable sea of revisionist detractors and eventually succeeded in doing so.

With close proximity to Scotland's capital, however, it was only a matter of time before he found himself engaging in the emerging world of Demarco's Edinburgh. A private man, he found an inner strength with his first wife Adrienne, their three children, and second wife Fritzy.

Dawyck Haig first exhibited his landscape paintings at the Demarco Gallery in 1968. Both Dawyck Haig and Joseph Beuys were fated to become prisoners of war as a result of the Battle of the Bulge after D-Day. Subsequent 'event photographs' in the Demarco Archive recall a string of EDINBURGH ARTS visits to Bemersyde featuring Demarco Gallery administrator Jane MacAllister, a young Daniel Day-Lewis wearing shorts, and the equally young long haired future designer of gardens Julian Bannerman.

Rosslyn Castle

With the storm of publicity surrounding the publication of the book and subsequent film of *The Da Vinci Code*, visitors to Rosslyn Chapel on the outskirts of Edinburgh are frequently unaware of the semi-ruined but still inhabited Rosslyn Castle in the adjacent Roslin Glen.

Yet it is more or less certain that the original castle, erected two centuries before the now world-famous chapel was built, stood on the same site. It was only after the now largely forgotten Battle of Roslin Glen in 1303 that a captured English prisoner generously suggested that a far less vulnerable spot for the seventh Lord of Rosslyn to have his stronghold would be on a rock promontory situated below.

Now this might sound a bit odd given that the recommended

location was on lower ground, but there is sufficient evidence to suggest that in the 14th century, the water level in the gorge of Roslin Glen was of sufficient height to have formed a lochan, and therefore, by building on the proposed rock, the castle would have been surrounded by water.

As the centuries passed, it seems that this expanse of water must have steadily dropped to the current level of the River North Esk, the frothy stream which rushes through the gorge from its source in the Pentland Hills. Certainly, the low-lying marshy land to the north-west of the castle is still known locally as The Stanks (which means 'Stagnant Pool'), and it encloses a small hillock known as The Goose's Mound.

Given the design of the castle – the five levels, the steep drop into the glen on all sides and the high arched drawbridge – this would all make perfect sense.

The story of the Viking-Norman-Anglo-Scots St Clairs of Rosslyn remains at the core of Scotland's history. It began in 1068 with the arrival of a young Norman knight known as William 'The Seemly', so called for his blond good looks and blue eyes. This William 'The Seemly' had accompanied the Saxon Princess Margaret Atheling in her escape from their mutual cousin William the Conqueror. When she married Malcolm III, King of Scots, in 1069, William 'The Seemly' was rewarded with a knighthood and the lands of Rosslyn which, then as now, guard the southern frontal approaches to Edinburgh.

In the generations that followed, his descendants prospered with his sons acquiring the lands of Pentland, and Herdmanston in East Lothian. Through a series of lucrative marriages, the St Clair Lords of Rosslyn and Pentland also became princes of Orkney and earls of Caithness and Strathearn, the latter earldom, a title which passed to the Royal House of Stewart and gifted by Her Majesty the Queen to her grandson on his marriage to Kate Middleton. On inheriting the Caithness earldom, a later branch of the St Clair family settled in the north of Scotland and founded Clan Sinclair.

But in theory the ownership of such titles and territories was all about the protection of the reigning monarch's interests and when it came to building a new castle in Roslin Glen, the St Clairs, with their Norman connections, knew exactly how to set about it. The availability of a large quantity of local sandstone was a bonus and the fortress which the St Clairs built most certainly came into its own when Edward II of England made incursions into Scotland between 1334 and 1337.

In 1369, a 25-year truce was negotiated between England and Scotland, but by then Henry St Clair, ninth Lord of Rosslyn, having become Prince of Orkney (inherited in 1379 through his grandmother), was becoming increasingly preoccupied with building Kirkwall Castle. He therefore left the day-to-day running of Rosslyn to his son, another Henry, and it was he who constructed the great dungeon and situated the five-storeys-high entrance on the far side of the inner courtyard. It is these levels which give the castle its lofty, unassailable appearance.

In 1420, the succession of William, 11th Lord of Rosslyn and third and last St Clair Prince of Orkney, yet again breathed new life into the castle with a spate of renovation work which included the creation of a bridge under the castle, and further fortifications. The greater part of the north-west wall remains, with buttresses to strengthen the height, but of the other proportions only massive chunks survive.

And it was this same William St Clair who embarked upon the building of the Church of St Matthew, better known today as Rosslyn Chapel. A complex individual, this William's lifespan encompassed the reigns of three Stewart monarchs – James I, James II and James III.

At the age of 21, he was made responsible for James I's 12-year-old daughter when she was sent off to marry the 13-year-old Dauphin, later Louis XI of France, and it was on this trip that he must have seen the Gothic interiors of Notre Dame in Paris and Chartres Cathedral. It was these masterpieces of their time that undoubtedly inspired him.

The work, importing skilled masons from throughout Europe, began in 1446. The under croft of the old castle being already in existence, the site on the top of the hill was in many ways just waiting to be occupied. But at the same time, William was not only improving Rosslyn Castle, but Ravenscraig Castle in Fife, which he had exchanged with James II for his earldom of Orkney. Progress on all three projects was therefore slow, and it took almost 40 years before the chapel that we see today was completed.

By his marriage to his first wife Margaret Douglas, a granddaughter of Robert II of Scotland, William had a son and four daughters. When Margaret died, he married Marjorie Sutherland of Dunbeath, a great-great granddaughter of Robert the Bruce, and had a further six sons and seven daughters. Thereafter he allegedly married for a third time and had further issue. One wonders when he found time to think about bricks and mortar?

And it is hardly surprising that by the time of his death in 1484, his funds were widely depleted. This, of course, left his son third son Oliver, the heir to Rosslyn, unable to complete his father's vision of a great cathedral, and the work was abandoned. What we therefore see today is simply the exquisite and beautifully crafted artwork in stone which is today's Rosslyn Chapel, but just think what a marvel it would have been had the project been completed.

Perhaps it was for the best because in the 17th century both Rosslyn Castle and its chapel were threatened from another quarter. The St Clair's were perceived as staunch Catholics and with the arrival of the Reformation, a mob from Edinburgh stormed the castle and destroyed much of its contents. Miraculously, despite the windows and alters of the chapel being decimated, the majority of the carvings survived.

In 1650 Rosslyn Castle once more came under siege when Oliver Cromwell, self-styled Lord Protector of England, invaded Scotland. This time, the castle walls were relentlessly bombarded by the canons of General George Monck and, in the aftermath, Sir John, 17th Lord of Rosslyn, was imprisoned. Strapped for cash, the castle was half mortgaged, then sold, but fortuitously recovered by Sir John's younger brother James, who succeeded him as 18th Lord.

In the generations that followed, the Rosslyn inheritance passed into the Wedderburn and Erskine families, the latter acquiring the earldom of Rosslyn in the early 19th century. From then onwards, the family's principle place of residence was at Dysart in Fife.

When Peter, seventh Earl of Rosslyn inherited the Rosslyn estate in 1977, he was preparing to embark upon a successful career in the Metropolitan Police Force. The maintenance of both castle and chapel, by then re-established as a working collegiate church, was naturally of major concern, especially when he found himself obliged to base himself in the south of England.

The solution was to place the castle in the capable hands of The Landmark Trust, a Charity founded in 1965 to rescue and restore historic buildings and make them available for holiday lettings.

In 2003, the spectacular success of Dan Brown's book *The Da Vinci Code*, its plot culminating in a visit to Rosslyn Chapel, created a sensation. Since then, a state-of-the-art visitor centre for the chapel has been opened, but if anything, the costs and pressures on the maintenance of such an ancient and fragile place have increased tenfold. All credit must go to the Countess Helen, an art historian with film star good looks who has presided over the Rosslyn Chapel Trust's astonishing refurbishment programme, not to mention fronting *A Treasure in Stone*, a superb BBC4 television documentary film and authoring/co-authoring several publications on the subject. Incidentally, Roddy Martine's book *Secrets of Rosslyn* (Birlinn), first published in 2006, has so far enjoyed four re-print editions.

As for Rosslyn Castle, with its spectacular drawing room overlooking the gorge of Roslin Glen, its ornate dining room, and sleeping accommodation for seven, it has rapidly become an immensely popular holiday venue on the outskirts of Scotland's capital.

Now it must be emphasised that the castle is NOT open to the general public as such and its privacy should be respected at all times. However, as part of a visit to Rosslyn Chapel, a most rewarding experience is to walk down the pathway to the castle drawbridge, then step down into Roslin Glen through the archway beneath, where the ancient castle rises steeply overhead to create a scene from a Gothic fantasy. The sensation is compounded when it emerges that the Devil himself is reputed to have ridden his horse up the side of the bridge.

Is it any wonder such luminaries as Queen Victoria, the poet William Wordsworth and his sister Dorothy, Robert Burns, Sir Walter Scott, and the painters Alexander Nasmyth and Richard Demarco found such a place irresistible?

Above: Joseph Beuys, in collaboration with his student, Johannes Stüttgen, considering three small pieces of paper with the first containing the question 'Where are the souls of?' The second containing the names of artists, particularly relevant to the Beuys action 'Celtic Kinloch Rannoch: The Scottish Symphony'. Over 30 names are listed, including those of Masaccio, Giotto, Fra Angelico, van Gogh, Rembrandt, William Nicholson (father of Ben Nicholson) and Malevich. Edinburgh College of Art, 1970, during the exhibition 'Strategy: Get Arts'.

Joseph Beuys 'action' at Edinburgh College of Art, as a 'Requiem for the Unknown Artist', Strategy Get Arts, 1970.

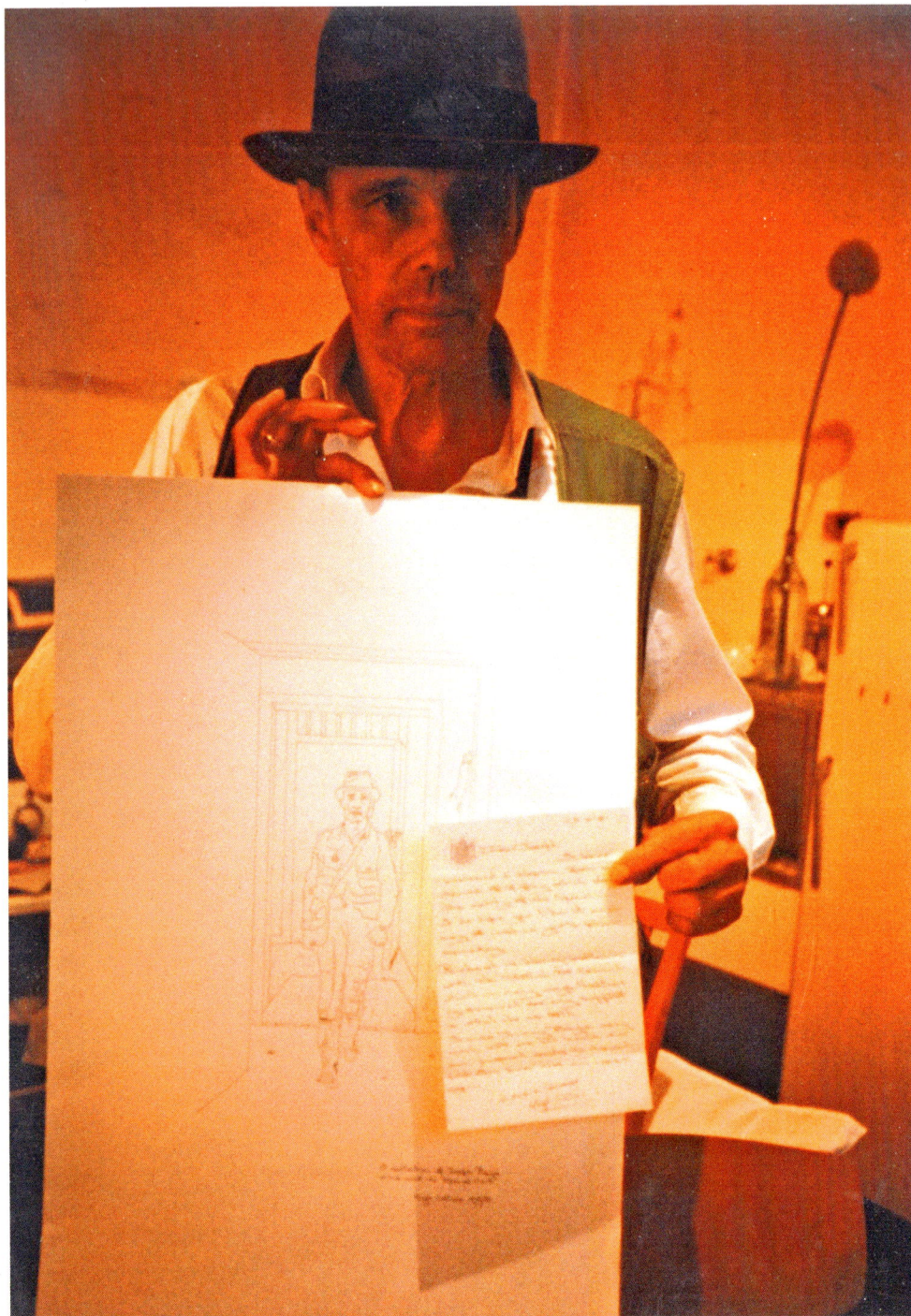

Hugh Collins' gift of a self-portrait to Joseph Beuys.

Joseph Beuys studying Edinburgh University's War Memorial, 1974.

The Danish sculptor-composer Henning Christiansen, in collaboration with his German wife, Ursula Reuter and the Scottish sculptor George Wyllie in their 'action' entitled '100 Hammer Blows against Warmongers'. This was commemorating the 25th anniversary of 'Strategy: Get Arts', 1995.

At the Forrest Hill Poorhouse, Paul Neagu's masterclass of his 'Going Tornado' for Edinburgh Arts, 1974.

The bronze head of Apollo in Ian and Sue Hamilton Finlay's garden of 'Little Sparta' in the Lanarkshire Hills inspired by the legend of Apollo, annually departing from his home in Delphi to fly towards to 'the land beyond where the North Wind blows' which Sandy Stoddart was commissioned to sculpt.

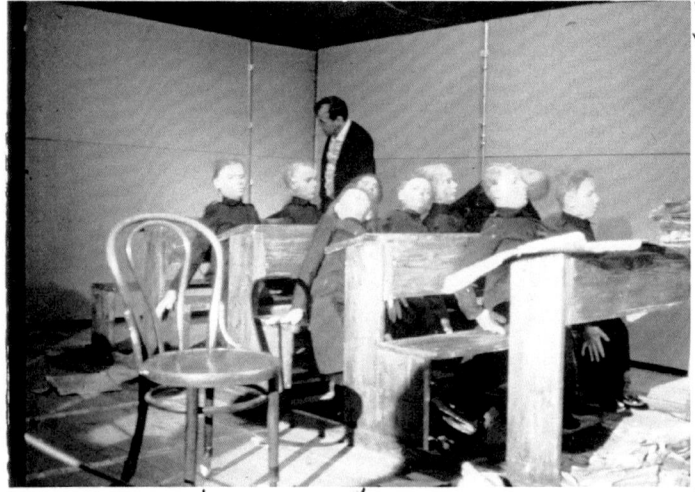

Handwritten annotations:
"EDINBURGH ARTS" '76 AT EDINBURGH College of Art

A DEMARCO GALLERY THEATRE PRODUCTION EDINBURGH FESTIVAL 1976

of POLISH School children in the EARLY PART OF THE CENTURY

TADEUSZ KANTOR WITH "THE DEAD CLASS" of MANNEQUINS — thin LIFE-LIKE sculptures

Tadeusz Kantor and his mannequins in the Cricot 2 production of 'The Dead Class' at Edinburgh College of Art, 1976.

Handwritten annotations:
1988 • EDINBURGH FESTIVAL DEMARCO THEATRE PRODUCTION FOR OFFICIAL FESTIVAL

"MACBETH" — A PRODUCTION OF SHAKESPEARE'S PLAY ON THE ISLAND OF INCHCOLM

AUDIENCE WATCHING "MACBETH"

DO WE SEE THE 3 WITCHES IN FULL DAYLIGHT !!?

The CHORISTERS PERCHED HIGH ON THE HILL OVERLOOKING INCHCOLM ABBEY

William Shakespeare's 'Three Witches' observe the Italian language production of the 'Scottish Play' performed in the ruined abbey on Inchcolm Island close to where the tragedy of Macbeth begins at the Battle of Kinghorn on the nearby Fife shoreline. The production was directed by Carlo Quartucci and Carla Tatò who played Lady Macbeth together with the Scottish actress Juliet Cadzow.

Andrew Marr at the private view of his paintings in the Demarco Wing of Robert McDowell's Summerhall Arts Centre in 2019. N.B. Alastair Darling, his Loretto School friend can be observed in the background.

Charlotte Rostek (left), the curator of Walter Dalkeith's 'Inception' exhibition at Dalkeith Palace in 2023. Richard Demarco in conversation with three of the artists, Jonathan Freemantle, Judy C Clark and Frippy Jameson. The discussion focused on the wide-ranging subject matter of the 'Inception' exhibition and how it has contributed to the rebirth of Dalkeith Palace.

Eva Kie, Izabella Brodzinska, Chair of the Scottish Polish Cultural Association, Claudia Zeiske, Richard Demarco, Roddy Martine, Terry Ann Newman, Marek Mutor, Deputy Director of the Ossoliński Institute of Poland, Sylwia Spooner from the Polish Consulate in Edinburgh, Professor Andy Lawrence and Colin Sanderson at Summerhall, 2023.

Roddy Martine's photograph of Richard Demarco and Catherine Maxwell Stuart during the 2023 Beyond Borders Festival at Traquair House in Peeblesshire, concluding a necessary political dimension to the three-week period of the Edinburgh Festival.

Terry Lane was the Artistic Director who had the responsibility of directing the highly successful programme of the Traverse Theatre in its inaugural year of 1963. This programme added an international dimension to the history of theatre in Scotland. This photograph by Roddy Martine was taken in Eddie Tait's Boardwalk Beach Cafe. This proved to be the ideal location for the launch of the Luath Press publication *Demarco's Edinburgh*. Eddie Tait has created an inspiring satellite of the Demarco Archive on the Promenade which leads to Cramond and its shoreline where, in 1972, the Demarco Gallery's *plein air* educational programme took place under the direction of Professor Tom Hudson.

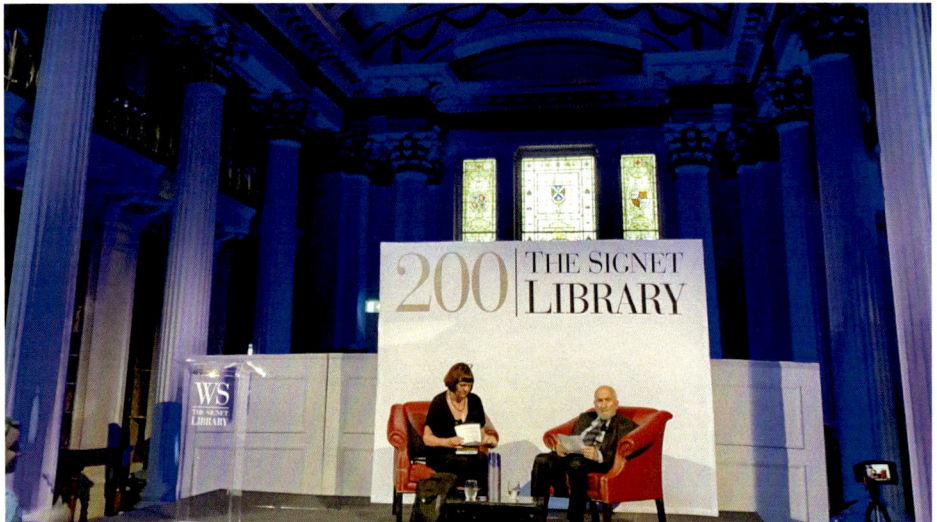

Richard Demarco in conversation with Amanda Catto, Director of the Visual Arts for Creative Scotland, during the celebration of the 200th anniversary of The Signet Library, Edinburgh Festival, 2022.

12

Renaissance men

THE EDINBURGH FESTIVAL WAS IN NEED OF THE WORLD OF THE TRAVERSE THEATRE

WHENEVER I THINK OF THE TRAVERSE THEATRE IN JAMES COURT I THINK OF MY CLOSE FRIENDS
TOM MICHELL, PETE MCGINN, MIKE MCLAUGHLIN, LORD (GEORGE) HARGWOOD, GRAHAM AUERBACH,
JOHN CALDER, JIM HAYNES, SHEILER SOLVIN, JOHN MARTIN, ANDY ELLIOT, TIMMY WINKER

JAMES CLOSE ~ THE HOME OF
THE ORIGINAL TRAVERSE THEATRE

Richard DemARco 92

John Calder

IN THE EARLY 1960s, it was the inspiration of the publisher John Calder to transform his family home at Milnathort in Fife to accommodate an arts festival. Born in Montreal, he was nonetheless a member of the Alloa-based Scottish brewing dynasty and in later years befriended the Irish dramatist Samuel Beckett. This led to his becoming the principal publisher of Beckett's prose-text poems in Britain when the stage production of *Waiting for Godot* became a runaway success in London in 1956. Calder further published the translated works of Anton Chekhov, Leo Tolstoy, Fyodor Dostoevsky, Amon Göth and Émil Zola. He was also the first to publish William S Burroughs in the UK.

With his roots now firmly in Scotland, Calder was a co-founder of the Traverse Theatre and with Sonia Orwell and Jim Haynes, devised and co-produced the International Writers' Conference in the McEwan Hall in 1962, followed by the Drama Conference of 1963.

That same year, he founded Ledlanet Nights which took place in the hall of the Calder family's mansion house in Kinross-shire. His life is candidly documented in detail in his autobiography *Pursuit: The Uncensored Memoirs of John Calder* (1999). Also revealed is the story of Ledlanet Nights.

Ledlanet Nights went from strength to strength, now having four seasons a year. Opera for All was back in 1968 and there were many small but good entertainments for all tastes during the year. Two operatic productions in the main autumn season, first of all a triple bill of Bach's only operatic work *The Coffee Cantata*, put into a sixties context. Britten's *Abraham and Isaac*, and a one-act comic opera by Joseph Horovitz, based on one of WS Gilbert's *Bab Ballads*, entitled *Gentleman's Island*. This had Ian Wallace and Stuart Kale in it and was much enjoyed.

Samuel Beckett's musical son Edward came with the Irish Chamber Orchestra.

'There was a brilliant performance of Walton's Façade with the Thorpe-Davie version of Burns' *Jolly Beggars*. The variety seems endless. There was Tom Stoppard's *Rosencrantz and Guildenstern*

Are Dead, and Lindsay Kemp's production of *Pierrot Lunaire*.'
By the start of the following decade, Calder was writing:

As Ledlanet continues through the early seventies, I tried to
give my audience not only as much of a variety as possible, but
a choice to hear as many of the greatest works of the concert
repertoire as I could. We did Bach's *Art of Fugue* and *Musical
Offering*, the Mozart *Requiem* in a programme that included
The Magic Flute... On one night Richard Demarco who was
running some kind of summer school, brought a bus load of
American girls, many of whom refused to leave in his bus.
'We're staying with the actors,' they said.

Sadly it seems that every visionary enterprise must have a beginning
and an end. In 1973, ambitious plans to increase the audience seating
from 150 to 600 seats in a theatre to be built behind the house were
scuttled by the advent of an expensive divorce from Calder's second
wife and the withdrawal of support from the Gulbenkian Foundation
and Scottish Arts Council. In retrospect, Calder reflected:

Certain years stand out in my memory with particular pain
and 1974 was one of them. The closure of Ledlanet was a
severe blow, but I was certain I would find a way of getting it
open again and, of course, our plans were well advanced for
the new building.

Alas, it was not to be.

Michael Spens

In 1975, at the invitation of Michael Spens, architect, publisher and
editor of *Studio International*, EDINBURGH ARTS first made a visit
to Cleish Castle, Kinross.
Cleish Castle is a sturdy 16th century tower house with 17th
century terraces, one of which is planted with an avenue of yew
trees. The land had come into the possession of Sir James Colville
of Ochiltree who passed it on to his son who built the castle. The

Colvilles were a rowdy lot, conspiring against James VI & I, taking part in the Ruthven Raid and later participating in an attack on the Palace of Holyroodhouse.

Therefore, it was not surprising that Cleish should be sold on and, by 1840, it had been allowed to become derelict. A reconstruction was undertaken by the Edinburgh architect John Lessels around 1870, then a remodelling took place in the 1970s.

Michael Spens lived an adventurous life committed to the history of ideas expressed essentially through the language of the visual arts. This began with the Second World War and its prolongation in the form of the Cold War.

He was rightly proud of his Scots ancestry which connected him to the medieval Scottish ballad of *Sir Patrick Spens*. This tells the story of the 13th century Scottish king, Alexander III, commanding his most skilful sailor, Sir Patrick Spens, to sail across the North Sea in winter to bring The Maid of Norway to Scotland, and how this princess was drowned, together with Sir Patrick Spens in tempestuous waters, 'full fifty fathoms deep' off the coast of Aberdeen.

It had been a visit to the Demarco Gallery in the early 1970s that made the connection between him and Richard, especially when Richard discovered he was meeting the successful young publisher of *Studio International*, the world's oldest and most prestigious arts journal. At this first encounter, they spoke of Michael's plans to restore a medieval castle located in The Cleish Hills near Dunfermline.

He saw this as the ideal home for his wife, Caroline, and their young family, allowing them to live their lives far from their terraced house in London's Belgravia. That first meeting also revealed the fact that Michael possessed a serious collection of modern art which included works by Scottish artists such as Eduardo Paolozzi and JD Fergusson, along with leading international artists such as Paul Klee, Claes Oldenberg and Henry Moore.

It was also inspiring that he chose Eduardo Paolozzi, then living and working in London. The commission was for The Great Hall at Cleish Castle and the resultant art work took the form of a thought-provoking, large-scale metal sculpture, a 20th-century version of the traditional painted wooden ceilings adorning many of Scotland's medieval castles. To this day, it can be seen installed high above the head of Paolozzi's gigantic statue of Vulcan, the Roman God of Fire and archetypal blacksmith, in the Scottish National Gallery of Modern Art. It was this major act of art patronage that convinced Michael to leave London and commit himself to the cultural, as well as political, life of Scotland.

For many years, he had been a much respected faculty member of Dundee University's School of Architecture. His spoken and written thoughts introduced his students to the world of landscape architecture, particularly to that of Sir Geoffrey Jellicoe, and to the world of international movements in general, including his wholehearted commitment to the iconic architecture of Alvar Aalto.

In the early 1990s, Michael contributed to the restoration of The Alvar Aalto Library, working in collaboration with Finnish and Russian authorities. It should be noted that the important nature of his work resulted in his being awarded a Finnish Knighthood in the form of The First Class Order of the Lion of Finland. This title befitted a Scot whose life had a distinct European dimension.

As a British Army officer stationed in Berlin during the Cold War, he had been involved in important military duties in the Middle East during the Suez Crisis. He had chosen to live his soldier's life in The Argyll and Sutherland Highlanders, the regiment that his father had served in with distinction during the Second World War and it was his deep regret that ill health prevented him from returning to the battleground of Monte Cassino.

Michael Spens was not only an architect, but a diplomat, a soldier, an art patron, an essayist, an art critic and inspiring teacher and lecturer and promoter of Scotland's culture throughout the international art world. Through meeting Richard Demarco, he accumulated many friends such as the Maltese art patron, poet and architect, Richard England, Murray Grigor, the film-maker, and in particular Hans Hollein, the Austrian architect. Hans Hollein was introduced to Scotland as a sculptor by Richard Demarco during the 1973 Edinburgh Festival.

The parkland surrounding Cleish Castle provided the ideal setting for an outdoor exhibition of large-scale metal sculpture by three Scottish artists he had championed, Gerald Ogilvie-Laing, Gavin Scobie and Andrew Myleus.

Richard introduced Michael to Arthur Sackler in 1980, which resulted in Sackler becoming the publisher of *Studio International* with Spens as editor. A few years later, Michael was invited by Nick Waterlow, a long-time friend of Richard's, and Director of the Arts

Council of Australia, to visit Australia to help plan an exhibition of Australian and New Zealand art entitled 'Anzart', to be mounted at Edinburgh College of Art for the Demarco Gallery in the 1984 Edinburgh International Festival.

In Australia, Michael met Janet McKenzie, the Australian artist, writer and acknowledged expert on the art of Arthur Boyd. Their subsequent marriage and collaboration as co-editors of *Studio International* following the death of Arthur Sackler, gave both the opportunity to expand their commitment and support of international artists and art institutions, defining the map of the international art world.

13

Fife to Fingask

OF COURSE THE THREE WISE KINGS WILL FOLLOW THE STAR OF BETHLEHEM TO THE COASTLINE OF PALESTINE AND ISRAEL. FROM THIS COASTLINE THE CELTS BEGAN THEIR VOYAGE TO THE KINGDOM OF DALRIADA AS A SACRED PLACE OF CORONATION OF THE KINGS OF SCOTLAND AND IRELAND

IT WAS PROFESSOR JOHN McQUEEN, AS DIRECTOR OF EDINBURGH UNIVERSITY'S SCHOOL OF SCOTTISH STUDIES DURING THE INAUGURAL VERSION IN 1972 OF THE DEMARCO GALLERY'S EDINBURGH ARTS PROGRAMME WHO STATED THIS HISTORICAL FACT

THE HISTORIC AND MYTHOLOGICAL VOYAGE IS EXPRESSED IN THE CELTIC STORY OF "TRISTAN AND ISEULT" ASSOCIATED WITH THE GERMANIC MYTHOLOGY OF "TRISTAN AND ISOLDE" MADE WORLD RENOWNED IN THE MUSIC OF WAGNER

THE 3 WISE KINGS FOLLOW THE CHRISTMAS STAR IN HOLYROOD ABBEY — R. DEMARCO '23

The Road to Bethlehem

INSPIRED BY HER Surrey-based parents Peter and Ann Hutley, Charlotte de Klee and her husband Rupert held their first Christmas Passion Play at their Lochiehead home, near Auchtermuchty, in 1994. Directed by Helen Molchanoff, it was a spectacular success.

During the 1980s, Peter and Ann had been on a visit to Medjugorje in the former Yugoslavia. With reported sightings of the Virgin Mary and having both been deeply influenced by the American novel and 1943 film *The Song of Bernadette*, they returned home to England to launch an annual Christmas Nativity play at their farm on the Wintershall estate.

From then on thousands have participated in this remarkable open-air nativity play in England and when Charlotte and Rupert found themselves living in Scotland, it seemed a logical progression to create a northern version and recruit the local community to participate in what rapidly evolved into an emotive winter pageant known as the Fife Nativity Play, taking place at different locations.

Charlotte recalls Richard Demarco as a bundle of charismatic energy. An unstoppable force of enthusiasm and encouragement. 'We usually meet Ricky (and Terry) travelling, M6 service station for a coffee at 7am in the morning when most folk are in bed,' she said. 'Art fairs moving up and down the isles, evaluating and assessing the talent. Ever ready to get out his camera for a quick photo opportunity. A record of his extraordinary life.'

'Ricky helped and supported all we did at Lochiehead,' she continued. 'His own personal deep faith and support for our Christian plays gave us confidence. He and Terry would show up unannounced and sit tucked up on a bale of straw in the barn as he watched the local aristocracy playing kings coming in on the local stables horses or the supportive farmers cajoling the sheep in the fields around the bonfires.

'We have Ricky's detailed paintings hanging in our home and we eagerly await his gallop of a newsletter reminding us of the meaning of the Twelve Days of Christmas. Life is never dull with Ricky about. I feel his life has enhanced ours in every way.'

Said Rupert, 'I first met Ricky in 1994 when I was asked by Father Jozo of Medjugorje, in Bosnia, to exhibit 30 Bosnian children's war time paintings to raise awareness of their plight. They were unsurprisingly harrowing images but, at the time, just on plain paper. The parish priest of Inverkeithing sent me to Ricky, then based off Albany Street, for advice.

'He was forthright, the paintings had to be framed appropriately. In turn he despatched me off to JR Smith in Dunfermline from whence they returned simply framed but ready for touring.

'"Don't do it unless you do it properly" became my abiding memory, no need to be an amateur!

'Since then, as for everybody, he has continued to pop up right across our lives, particularly supporting the Nativity and Passion plays at Lochiehead, outside Auchtermuchty which, vitally for him, sat right on the pilgrim's route between Meikle Seggie and St Andrews Cathedral.

Fingask Castle

In the foothills of the Sidlaws, between Perth and Dundee, with leisurely views to the south over the Carse of Gowrie to the Firth of Tay, Fingask Castle rises unexpectedly from the woodland like a châteaux in a fairy-tale. In a distant time, pilgrims and Scottish kings paused here to pray at St Peter's Well in the adjacent dell before journeying on to Scone, or to the shrine of the saintly Queen Margaret at Dunfermline. A marker still carries the lines:

Drink, weary pilgrim, drink.
And bless St Peter's well
Unscathed by sun or scorching ray,
Or frost or thawing swell.

All around there is rich agricultural land which, with a southerly outlook and low rainfall, makes this corner of rustic Perthshire perfect for fruit growing, hence strawberries and raspberries are integral to the local economy. But the demands of owning and maintaining a historic country house are constant, and the Fingask estate has seen more than its fair share of highs and lows.

A castle certainly existed here as early as the reign of Alexander I in the 12th century, but little is known of its early history until the 15th century when it passed into the hands of the Bruce family who held a Charter for the lands of Rait. These Bruces belonged to the senior line of the Bruces of Clackmannan, descended from a nephew of Scotland's hero King Robert the Bruce, and a stone in the house records their having been here in 1594. However, family fortunes rise and fall, and by 1671 the last of the Bruce lairds of Fingask was obliged to sell to settle his 'pecuniary involvements'.

The new owners, the Threipland family, who derived their name from a vale in the parish of Kilbucho in Peeblesshire, renovated the existing house and laid out the gardens. In 1674, Patrick Threipland was knighted for his diligence in the suppression of the Covenanters, and in 1687 he was created a Baron of Nova Scotia.

Alas, disrupting forces were at work throughout the land. The politics of the 17th century divided Scotland in a succession of devastating conflicts. When the Stuart monarch James VIII fled into exile, he was supplanted on the British throne by his daughter Mary and son-in-law William of Orange, thus bringing to an end the hereditary rule of the House of Stuart. The Threiplands, in common with so many of Scotland's old families – the Erskines, the Setons, the Gordons and the Keiths – took up arms in support of their exiled monarch's Jacobite Cause, and consequently paid the price. Sir Patrick died in Stirling Castle where he was held a prisoner, and his son Sir David, having fought at the Battle of Sheriffmuir, had his baronetcy attainted and family properties confiscated.

As was the fate of so many other Jacobite properties, Fingask was compulsorily purchased from the Government by the York Buildings Company which held on to it until 1782, albeit leasing it to Sir David's second wife, Dame Katherine.

Dame Katherine was a doughty matriarch who gave birth to a baby boy during the castle's occupation by Hanoverian troops. The captain in charge of the troops sent word to her asking what she wanted the boy christened. 'Stuart' came the terse reply.

In the subsequent Rising of 1745, Sir Stuart, now qualified as a physician, became Bonnie Prince Charlie's personal physician. After the disastrous Battle of Culloden the following year, he found himself alone and lost on the moors and was about to fall into a nest of redcoats when, according to his story, an angel came down and told him not to go that way, but to follow a different path to where a group of fleeing Jacobites could be found.

This apparition had such an effect on Sir Stuart that he 20 years later commissioned the French artist Eugène Delacroix to immortalise the occasion. The picture is now in the collection of the National Galleries of Scotland and is displayed in their gallery at Duff House, near Banff. By 1783, the Jacobite threat was minimal and the Government allowed exiles to come home.

Sir Stuart, with a price on his head, and not unlike Jamie Fraser, the hero of Diana Gabaldon's bestselling *Outlander* novels, had sought anonymity as a doctor in the old town of Edinburgh. He latterly became an early President of the Royal College of Physicians. His medical chest can be still seen in the society's palatial headquarters.

The York Building Company filed for bankruptcy in 1783, and a sale of the confiscated estates which the company had bought from the Government took place. The story goes that the 'rightful heirs of the Jacobite estates formed a ring at the auction by hiring some rough looking Highlanders to keep all bidders apart from the old Jacobites out'. By this means, Sir Stuart was able to buy back the Threipland's castle and estates of Fingask.

It says a lot about the resilience of bloodlines. In 1826, Stuart's son Patrick, after adopting the Budge and Murray surnames from whom his mother's wealth was inherited, had the family baronetcy restored by Act of Parliament. It was he who made the additions to the west-facing front of the castle, also building onto the south front. Contemporary accounts such as the recently published *The Butler's Day Book*, give an amusing account of the day-to-day preoccupations of the household.

In 1882, the property passed to a cousin, Colonel William Scott Kerr of Roxburgh, who assumed the surname of Murray Threipland. He and his wife owned other properties in England and Wales and, in 1917, sold the estate to Sir John Henderson Stewart, a prosperous Dundonian Scotch whisky merchant. A casualty of prohibition, Sir John died in 1925 owing a spectacular £570,000 which meant that once again Fingask was up for grabs.

This time, the estate, which at this juncture comprised 2587 acres, was bought by the Gilroy family of Ballumbie, a neighbouring Angus estate, who demolished the 19th-century additions. In 1969, the estate, by now reduced to 75 acres, was returned to the Threipland family when it was bought by William Murray Threipland's grandson Mark, and then in 1995, purchased from him by his brother Andrew Murray Threipland, the current Laird.

Andrew and his wife Helen are an engaging couple. With their talented children, Peter, Sacha and Beatrice, Fingask Castle is once again a family home. It is not often a house has been lost and bought back by the same family four times.

In keeping with the family motto: *Animis et Fato* ('By courageous acts and good fortune'), the Threiplands have persevered. Film and theatre director Helen Threipland, born Helen Molchanoff, whose Petrograd (St Petersburg) family had fled from the Bolsheviks to London in 1924, has kept up her family's spirit by introducing an exquisite Russian Orthodox Chapel. With the elegantly situated Pavilion on the Lawn, Fingask Castle today plays host to a series of weddings, receptions and highly entertaining and eccentric events.

The Fingask Follies, a musical review conceived by Andrew and Helen, takes place in May, and is now in its 28th year. A light-hearted and themed comedy and song extravaganza, it is scripted by the Threiplands and Andrew's lifelong friend Nigel 'Lofty' Buchanan. Such is the demand for tickets that it now goes on tour to venues in Edinburgh, Glasgow, as far south as London and this year, Geneva.

One of the great joys of visiting Fingask on a summer day, or indeed at any time of year, is to take a leisurely stroll through its topiary gardens and encounter the statuary hidden among the many picturesque, secluded walkways. There is a hilarious group of carved figures from Scots literature by the Victorian stone mason David Anderson from Perth, and characters from the works of Alexander Thomson, Robert Burns and Sir Walter Scott; also a full-length statue of the British prime minister William Pitt the Younger, a naked black figure of Doryphoros, some small pieces by Charles Spence and a head by the contemporary sculptor Sandy Stoddart.

The Highland Shakespeare Touring Company with Richard Demarco as patron was launched here following a production of *The Tempest* in 2013 at the Edinburgh Festival, and led to glorious out-of-doors performances at the Belladrum Tartan Heart Festival, near Inverness, at Cambo House in Fife and in the gardens of Fingask Castle, with multi-lingual productions of *A Midsummer Night's Dream* in French, Russian, German, Arabic and Luxembourgish taking place on Inchcolm Island, and now annually in the Dean Gardens of Edinburgh with audiences taken on a musical and spiritual journey into the magical other world below Thomas Telford's iconic Dean bridge.

Conceived by the dashing film-maker and actor-manager Sunny Moodie and his beautiful sister, composer and clarsach musician Siannie Moodie, Highland storyteller Lizzie McDougall and Helen Molchanoff, the diverse and aesthetically captivating young cast conjure up fantastical spectacles against the backdrop of the natural landscape.

The Highland Shakespeare Company was born to answer the call led by Richard Demarco to reimagine the hit Edinburgh Festivals show *The Tempest* at Hopetoun estate and take it on tour. The touring production saw a cast and crew of over 20 persons bring Shakespeare's masterpiece to critical acclaim and sell out audiences at Fingask Castle and Belladrum Estate. Demarco was there from the beginning; inspiring and encouraging the young company.

On any given day he could be found giving masterclasses on interpreting Shakespeare's text, deep in intellectual discussions on the nature of theatre or leading the company out on adventures into the physical landscape of Scotland. In the morning he could be found contextualising the company's contributions to the Edinburgh Festivals with reference to The Greats he had witnessed over the decades, and in the afternoon he would be explaining the relevance of Shakespeare's poetry to the life of the arts in Scotland, and its meaning to The Road to Meikle Seggie.

Under such an illuminating artistic aegis the company felt the confidence to give its all to the productions it staged. After The Tempest on Tour, The HSC brought an enchanting *A Midwinter Night's Dream* to the snowdrop gardens at Cambo Estate and then to Fingask Castle. The audience were transported to a Shakespearian winter wonderland and *The Scotsman* newspaper gave it four stars and a glowing review. The full moon that night played its part well, coming out from behind the clouds just in time for Oberon's address to Titania, 'met by moonlight'.

Following this production The Highland Shakespeare Company staged *The Dream* on Inchcolm Island. The audience travelled to the island on a boat alongside actors placed in disguise in their midst. As the ship docked at the island the actors threw off their disguises, revealed as brave Athenians who brought the audience ashore where they were greeted by the call of the Carnyx and an island that came to life all around them with actors and music.

The company assembled again to stage a special birthday performance for Richard Demarco. This play grew to become *All The World's a Stage* which was presented at the Dean Gardens in Edinburgh later that year as part of the Edinburgh Festivals.

The play *All The World's A Stage* was Shakespeare in seven different languages, translated by some of the world's foremost poets to give the audience experiences such as *Romeo and Juliet* in French and *Oberon and Titania* in Arabic. Later productions have included *Protect The Flame* which staged Richard Demarco's fabled meeting with Joseph Beuys and *Searching for The Timeless* where the audience followed Puck and Pan to an Arcadia of music and theatre.

The Company has also made a number of pieces of cinema. These include *Wild Hearts*, an entirely Shakespearian feature length script assembled to tell the legend of Apollo and Daphne which was presented as part of the Venice Biennale Film Festival and *Nighean Na Coille*, an enchanting telling of the coming of St Bride that won awards in California.

In total, hundreds of individuals including poets, actors, musicians, artists, writers, costume designers and film makers have contributed to the life of The Highland Shakespeare Company.

Sunny McDougall Moodie, actor-manager of The Highland Shakespeare Company commented: 'For me Ricky's tremendous love and support, encouragement and inspiring creative dynamism have always been at the heart of The Highland Shakespeare Company, for which I am eternally grateful.'

An unexpected leafy oasis on the eastern extremities of eastern Perthshire, Fingask Castle envelopes its visitors in a cloak of beauty and enchantment, and continually springs to life with the energy of its occupants. There is an awful lot to be said for the commitment of 400 years of dynastic love. Above a doorway on the first landing is a trompe l'oeil in celebration of the tenth decade of the Life of Chevalier Richard Demarco CBE.

14

Ravenscraig, Auchinleck and The Binns

AT THE BEGINNING OF THE
EDINBURGH ART
EXPEDITION FROM
BUDAPEST TO
TIMISOARA

FROM
HUNGARY
TO
ROMANIA

THE WINDMILL'S SAILS

8.15AM 19/3 R.DEMARCO
TO 8.25AM 19/91

I REGARD THIS PEN DRAWING AS AN IMAGE OF EUROPE AS CHRISTENDOM.

BELOW THE
CRUCIFIX IS A
STATUE OF MARY AT THE
—GRIEVING AT THE
DEATH OF SON

A PIECE OF ROADSIDE
RELIGIOUS SCULPTURE
UNTHINKABLE ON
THE OUTSKIRTS
OF BRITAIN'S
LATE 20TH CENTURY CITIES!!!

ON THE OUTSKIRTS OF AVONPORT IN THE SMALL TOWN OF KECSKEMET
THERE IS AN INN. IDEAL FOR BREAKFAST. THE INN HAS A MATERIAL
ROOF. AND BESIDE IT IS A CROSS WITH THE CRUCIFIED CHRIST
— ERECTED BESIDE A WORKING WINDMILL. — I DREW THIS AS A
NODAL POINT ON THE ROAD TO MEIKLE SEGGIE BEGINNING IN SCOTLAND

That Scottish Play again

RAVENSCRAIG CASTLE WAS one of the star turns of the 1996 Edinburgh Festival when The Scottish Play was enacted on its battlements before an enraptured audience seated on a windswept clifftop overlooking on one side the public park of the linoleum town of Kirkcaldy; on the other, the North Sea.

Strategically situated on Scotland's east coast, with its canons commanding the mouth of the Firth of Forth, Ravenscraig Castle was considered to be an immensely important addition to the defences of the Scottish realm. The Scots had previously been attacked from the sea by the Vikings, and during the Wars of Independence when Robert the Bruce was absent fighting in Ireland. From the 14th century onwards a string of North Sea outlook fortresses were purpose-built from Berwick to Wick. From Eyemouth to North Berwick, the horizons were constantly being watched from the battlements of castles at Dunbar, Fast and Tantallon.

Across the Firth of Forth, on the northern Fife coast, was the formidable Bishop's Palace of St Andrews. At Stonehaven there was Dunottar, and at Cruden Bay, Slains Castle. In Caithness, serving the interests of the Norse/Norman/Scots family of St Clair, were the formidable castles of Dunbeath, Girnigoe and Sinclair, and Keiss.

It was James II of Scotland who in the spring of 1460 gave instructions to build a sea fort at Ravenscraig. Alas, he was soon after killed by an exploding canon at the Siege of Roxburgh Castle in the Scottish Borders. It was at the partly built Ravenscraig Castle, however, that his widow Mary of Gueldres, decided to take up residence after his death.

King James II considered his designs for Ravenscraig Castle to be among his proudest achievements. His son James III, having completed the building work after his father's death, had another agenda in mind.

On his marriage to Princess Margaret of Denmark in 1409, he had been given the Orkney and Shetland Isles as a dowry settlement. However, the Jarldom of Orkney, which comprised the Northern Isles of Scotland, remained through marriage, with the St Clairs. The position of Jarl (Earl) of Orkney was in effect the most senior rank in medieval Norway next to the King. At the same time, the St Clairs were subjects of the Scottish Crown.

In 1470, King James offered Ravenscraig Castle and its adjoining land and an annual pension of 40 marks to Prince William St Clair in exchange for the Norse earldom of Orkney. Since Prince William was also the 11th Baron of Rosslyn, this was a Royal Command and he had little option but to accept the offer. Twenty years earlier William had also agreed to swap the wealthy earldom of Nithsdale for the less profitable earldom of Caithness. In such a manner were Scotland's medieval economy and spheres of influence kept under control.

Oliver Cromwell invaded Scotland in the mid-17th century and Ravenscraig was seriously damaged by the English army. Nevertheless, the Dysart estate, and what remained of the castle, stayed under St Clair/St Clair-Erskine/Sinclair ownership until 1898 when the gambling debts of the popular but financially inept fifth Earl of Rosslyn caught up with him. All of his Fife properties were sold to the linoleum magnate Sir Michael Nairn, who took up residence at Dysart House.

Time moves on relentlessly and in 1955 the ruins of Ravenscraig Castle were taken into care by Historic Scotland.

During the Edinburgh Festival of 1996, made possible through a grant of £30,000 from the British Council's Department of Visiting Arts, the Belarus State Theatre in collaboration with Fife College, directed by Valerie Anisenko, and with Yelena Schellenberg in the role of Lady Macbeth, performed William Shakespeare's masterpiece in Belarusian to an open-air audience on the clifftop, snuggled up under blankets and umbrellas.

Although the majority of those who were there did not understand a spoken word, they all knew the plot. The only word to aptly describe the experience was 'ethereal'.

What you are looking for is here

The first recorded member of the Boswell family arrived in Britain with the Norman invasion of 1066 and was identified as having originated from the town of Beauzeville in France. It is uncertain exactly when they arrived in Scotland but the name emerged in the following centuries as being established at Balmuto in Fife. In 1504, Thomas Boswell of the Balmuto family married the daughter and heiress of Sir John Auchinleck of that Ilk. The union was enthusiastically endorsed by King James IV, so they must have become established by then.

Thomas was to die alongside his king on the battlefield of Flodden in 1513. Up until then, the Auchinleck family had occupied a castle situated high up on a crag, moving to an equally defensible site and the ruins of that fortified house can still be seen. In 1591, John Boswell, grandson of Thomas, was exposed as a necromancer and obliged to flee the country. Thereafter his family kept a low profile with at least two of them allegedly suffering from mental diseases, but in 1754, Alexander, eight Laird of Auchinleck, was appointed to the Court of Session, taking the judicial title of Lord Auchinleck.

With family fortunes on the rise, it was he who decided to commission a mansion, the design of which he is said to have orchestrated himself. Certainly a major influence must have been neighbouring Dumfries House which had recently been built by the Earl of Dumfries, and which has now passed to the Great Steward of Scotland's Trust, presided over by King Charles III.

Auchinleck House was therefore an undeniable confirmation of status. Above the front entrance is a frieze with symbols illustrating the vocations of Lord Auchinleck, his brother and his sons; music, martial arts, scales of justice, a sceptre of authority and the serpent-entwined staff of Asclepius the Healer, are grouped around the central motif, a hooded falcon deriving from the Boswell family crest. Carved into the stone in Latin are the words of the Roman lyric poet Horace: 'Quad Petus hic est, est ulubris, animus sic e non deficit aequus,' translated as 'What you are looking for is here at Ulubrae, if only balance on mind does not desert you.'

However, while Lord Auchinleck concentrated on his distinguished legal career, commuting between Ayrshire and Edinburgh, his relationship with his eldest son and heir became increasingly strained. The young James Boswell, like all young juveniles rebelling against parents to seek out the bright lights of London, was dismissive of their Calvinist attitudes and while in London fell under the spell of the towering figure of Dr Samuel Johnson, compiler of *The Dictionary of the English Language,* and arguably considered to be one of the most outstanding living men of letters in Hanoverian England.

Johnson was 31 years older than the sycophantic James, but their friendship blossomed and in 1773 they set off together upon what was to become a legendary tour of the Scottish Hebrides, a collaboration that is remarked upon to this day. Both men left published accounts which were to become bestsellers. At the end of their adventure, James brought his friend to stay at Auchinleck House where Dr Johnson, a devout Anglican, and Lord Auchinleck, a strict Presbyterian, famously argued bitterly over politics in the library. According to the records both men enjoyed themselves immensely.

Ever in the shadow of his father, James Boswell's legal career continued to flounder until his death at the age of 54, but his greatest achievement was his towering biography of Samuel Johnson, published after the deaths of both his friend and his father.

The Auchinleck estate remained with the immediate Boswell family until it passed through marriage through the female line to the Irish Malahide family. In the 1920s, Talbot de Malahide sold the state to his cousin Lt Colonel John Douglas Boswell.

During the Second World War, Auchinleck House was occupied by officers from the armies of Poland, Canada and France. In 1996, it was handed over by the current James Boswell to the Scottish Historic Buildings Trust which ensured its survival. In 1999, Auchinleck House was acquired by The Landmark Trust, the historic building preservation society, and can now be leased for accommodation and specific events. In recent years, the Boswell family has launched Boswell's Coach House, a popular farm shop and coffee stop within the confines of the Auchinleck estate.

The Muskovite Devil

Dating from the 17th century with the inevitable 18th and 19th century additions, the House of The Binns is located on 200 acres of parkland and so named from its location on a 'Ben', the Celtic word for 'hill', was for generations occupied by the Dalyell family. In 1944, it was gifted to the National Trust for Scotland by Eleanor, the mother of the well-known Labour member of Parliament for West Lothian Tam Dalyell, a man of great integrity and decency. Until his retirement in 2005, the individualistic and outspoken Tam Dalyell was revered as Father of the House of Commons, and nothing more aptly summed him up than the title of his biography *The Importance of Being Awkward* (Mainstream, 2000).

It was his mother who was the Dalyell, with his father adopting her maiden name, and he was a sixth cousin of the American President Harry S Truman who descended from the daughter of the first Dalyell of The Binns Baronet. The family's fortunes began more than 400 years ago when another Tam Dalyell, an Edinburgh-based butter merchant, travelled to London in 1603 to join the Court of James VI of Scotland when he was crowned King James I of England. As a relative of the earls of Carnwath, and married to a daughter of Lord Bruce of Kinloss, Master of the King's Rolls, he was well connected and prospered accordingly. In 1612, to capitalise on his success, he acquired the Bynnis Estate and began the building of the House of The Binns. It was on this estate in 1681 that his son, General Tam Dalyell, raised the Royal Scots Greys regiment.

An impassioned Royalist supporter, he was ruthless in pursuit of his enemies and it was not long before he acquired the nickname of 'Bloody Tam' and subsequently 'Muscovite devil.' His military career began at the age of 13 when he took part in Charles I's expedition to La Rochelle. He later served with the Royal Army in Ulster under General Munro and General Leslie.

On hearing of the execution of Charles I in 1649, he was sufficiently disgusted to avow that as a penance for his fellow countrymen having allowed this to take place, he would never again shave his beard. Taken prisoner by the Commonwealth Army, he was grudgingly released but obliged to remain in Ulster until the following year when he rallied to the support of Charles II at the Battle of Worcester. Captured once again, he was imprisoned in the Tower of London but managed to escape abroad, returning three years later to lead an abortive uprising in the Highlands.

With a reward of 200 guineas for his capture, dead or alive, he set off for Russia where he entered the service of the Tsar and fought against the Turks and Tartars. With the restoration of Charles II, he returned to Britain and in 1666 was appointed Commander in Chief of the Army in Scotland with specific instructions to suppress the growing support for the Covenanting movement which opposed the Anglican prayer book. This he pursued with ruthless efficiency at the Battle of Rullion Green at which 1200 prisoners were taken and corralled in Greyfriars Kirkyard in Edinburgh. He was merciless. It was he who introduced the thumbscrew as an instrument of torture, and the spectre of Bloody Tam has lingered in the Scottish psyche ever since. However, his descendant Tam of Westminster remains in the hearts of all who knew him.

15

Stonypath and Kinloch Rannoch

The Estonian Youth Theatre

ROMEO

AND JULIET

DEATH

THIS PRODUCTION IS TAILOR-MADE FOR THE 1994 PROGRAMME OF THEATRE

I ENVISAGE IT IN THE COURTYARD OR TO DUNDEE SCHOOL OR PERHAPS OF ST MARY'S R.C. PRIMARY SCHOOL

CAN I BRING THE ESTONIAN YOUTH THEATRE BACK TO EDINBURGH WITH THEIR PRODUCTION OF SHAKESPEARE'S ROMEO & JULIET??

KIERKEGAARD

AT LITTLE SPARTA OR AS PART OF THE GARDEN ROUTE TO THE EDINBURGH FESTIVAL 1995

AND PERFORMED AT DUNDEE REP. DIRECTED BY SUE POGSON

ALL WOMEN AND YOU'RE A FEW WOMEN ARE RIGHT! ACCORDING TO ROGER POOLE! A PLAY INSPIRED BY KIERKEGAARD'S LOVE FOR REGINE OLSEN

THE PLAY READING WAS 'AT LITTLE SPARTA' AT THE INVITATION OF IAN HAMILTON FINLAY

THE 1995 EDINBURGH FESTIVAL

THIS WOULD BE AN ESTONIAN-LANGUAGE PRODUCTION.

Little Sparta

WHAT EXACTLY IS Concrete Poetry?

By definition it embraces 'objects composed of letters, words, colours and typefaces in which graphic space exercises a central role in both design and meaning.'

That said, Concrete Poets are renowned for experimenting boldly with language, incorporating visual, verbal, kinetic and sonic elements. Emerging during the 1950s as an art form in Northern Europe and South America, works of concrete poetry are considered to be as much representations of visual words as they are works of poetry.

Thus it was a solo exhibition held at the Demarco Gallery in 1969 that led Ian Hamilton Finlay to collaborate with a group of Mexican artists who were exhibiting works of concrete poetry in celebration of the Mediterranean island of Malta's heroic role in the Second World War. The impact on Hamilton Finlay's imagination was explosive. The rest is history.

Hamilton Finlay remains an enigma of his own making with a practical and often explosive instinct for survival. Born in the Bahamas, his parents brought him home to Scotland where he thereafter moved randomly about between Clackmannan, Glasgow, London and Kirkcudbright before National Service claimed him. Settling after this in Perthshire with his first wife Marion (Hugh MacDiarmid was best man at their wedding), he worked part-time as a shepherd and this was where he began to write short stories and poems.

Having set up the Wild Hawthorn Press with Jessie McGuffy, he published *Rapel* and his own magazine *Poor. Old. Tired. Horse.* (*P.O.T.H.*). It was over this period, that he claimed to have succumbed to a Northern Sensibility as distinct from Scots and Gaelic culture. He wrote prolifically, producing a series of semantically precise verses encapsulating his personal interaction with the world around him.

By 1966, he had met his second wife Sue Macdonald Lockhart and they soon after settled in the rural farmstead of Stonypath at Dunsyre, on the Lee and Carnwath estate, owned by her parents south of Edinburgh. In the creation of a garden at the heart of agricultural Lanarkshire, he and Sue were equally complicit.

With modest grants from the Scottish Arts Council, Hamilton Finlay began working on different collaborations of stone, neon and glass. He turned the dairy into a workshop with a gallery above to display prints. As Sue recalled, 'In time Ian saw the garden as another place to display his works in stone and wood.'

After that, Little Sparta, was created 'one turf at a time.'

From then on, the garden in bloom fell under Hamilton Finlay's esoteric fascination with the French Revolution, Heroic Emblems, the legacy of Germany's Third Reich Revisited and modernism. A pathway of russet-coloured flagstones, each imprinted with the word 'pretty' leads into a shady copse, a signpost marked 'Siegfried Line' points toward the corner of a field where washing is hung out to dry. A notice under thriving wild cherry trees carries the ironic message, 'Bring Back the Birch!'

In this poet's garden, conceived in the tradition of 18th century landscape gardeners Alexander Pope and William Shenstone, classical columns stand beside a series of ponds and planted areas, where inscriptions and a pair of garden temples have been placed to beguile and instruct. At the Temple of Apollo, visitors are invited to pay homage to the little drummer boy Barra who was killed by the Royalists during the French Revolution, a tragic event immortalised by Jacques-Louis David. A metal tortoise is inscribed 'Panther Leader'. Huge granite slabs reflect the seasons and are carved with the words of Louis Antoine de Saint-Just: 'The present order is the disorder of the future.'

In the late 1970s, he was commissioned to create a monumental project for the Max Planck Institute Garden in Stuttgart, Germany; similarly the Kröller-Müller Museum in Holland. An exhibition at the Serpentine Garden in London consolidated his status as an internationally inventive and respected artist.

No stranger to controversy, in 1978 he embarked upon a series of publicly staged confrontations with entrenched authority, whom he regarded as morally and intellectually bankrupt. A confrontation with Strathclyde Regional Council over the conversion of an outbuilding into a temple and whether or not this ought to be taxed as a religious building, was much publicised internationally and led to a string of European commissions with Hamilton Finlay being shortlisted for the Turner Prize.

Two remarkable achievements towards the end of his life in 2006, were the Improvement Garden installed at the Stockwood Discovery Centre at Luton, and the private Fleur de l'Air Garden in Provence, France.

It is in record that the name Little Sparta was chosen by Hamilton Finlay in 1983 in response to Edinburgh being tagged The Athens of the North, being set upon seven hills, and playing into the rivalry between the Ancient Greek cities of Athens and Sparta. As a Concrete Poet, he was ever conscious of the interplay of words. When Roddy Martine wrote the text for a coffee table book *Living in Scotland*, published in 1986, he titled the chapter on Little Sparta, 'An Eccentric Oasis'. On receipt of the page proofs, he received an animated late-night telephone call from Hamilton Finlay who defiantly insisted it be renamed 'An Oasis of Tradition'. It was a much more appropriate compromise.

Celtic (Kinloch Rannoch) the Scottish Symphony

The triumphant arrival of the internationally renowned German artist Joseph Beuys in Scotland has been well documented, not least in *Demarco's Edinburgh*. From the moment he first set foot in the Highlands in 1970, Beuys was inspired to concentrate on the physical reality of Scotland, the stuff and substance of its extraordinary landscape and its breathtaking cultural heritage.

So where did the pilgrimage of Joseph Beuys begin? On Rannoch Moor, of course. His passionate commitment to the Celtic world thereafter was to change the course of his life's work.

What was so special about this remote, inhospitable triangle of 50 square miles of boggy peat moorland festering in northerly Lochaber? At an altitude of 1,000 feet, why was it designated a Site of Special Scientific Interest and a Special Area of Conservation?

The answer is that its scenic origins lie in the last significant ice field in the Ice Age of continental Europe.

There had to be more to its existence than it simply being the homeland of the fictional Clan MacDuck, the documented ancestors of Walt Disney's Scrooge McDuck, Donald Duck's ancestor.

Bleak, moody, magnificent, dotted with lochans encircled by mountains, some rising to 3,000 feet. It is undeniable that the great moor of Rannoch is a vast time capsule. Above all, Rannoch Moor is spiritually inspirational. You sense this in the wind and in the rain on your face, and in the soft sunlight and sudden darkening of the skies. The landscape is regularly subject to multiple weather patterns in one day.

In Western literature, David Balfour and Alan Breck Stewart passed this way in Robert Louis Stevenson's *Kidnapped*; JK Rowling's *Harry Potter* and the casts of Irvine Welsh's *Trainspotting* and Diana Gabaldon's *Outlander,* have all manifested themselves in such a place.

It is therefore hardly surprising that Beuys, the co-founder of Germany's Green Party, should so unconditionally fall under the Celtic spell of this great expanse of lonely, hostile moorland. The camera catches his solitary, slender figure, a vagrant, gaunt scarecrow, traversing the windswept vista under a big and irrational sky. Only amid such surroundings is the futility of mankind's obsession with being in control put into perspective; in Beuys' own words, 'this sacred place that defies the human presence.'

For Beuys, Scotland's Celtic culture meshed inextricably with his belief in a less rational, less materialistic approach to living. Rannoch Moor became his muse. That same year, his electrifying Edinburgh performance show, *Celtic (Kinloch Rannoch) the Scottish Symphony*, in collaboration with the Danish Fluxus composer Henning Christiansen and Rory McEwen, bore lasting testament to his commitment.

Of course, there were others involved who were not part of the British art world. His students, Ute Klophaus and Johannes Stüttgen from the Kunstakademie in Düsseldorf, joined forces with the American painter of skies Jon Schueler. There was Mark Littlewood who was invited to film the surface of the Moor of Rannoch. In the *Scotsman*, the novelist Michael Pye wrote an account of the Beuys family's journey (Eva Beuys and their children Jessyka and Wenzel) travelling in Henry Gough-Cooper's rented white Mercedes, followed by Richard Demarco and his then assistant Lesley Benyon, in a blue Mini Traveller, and Rory McEwen and Mark Littlewood bringing up the rear.

On a gelatine covered wall at Edinburgh College of Art, Johannes Stüttgen posted up three messages. The first read, 'Where are the souls of...?'

The second piece of paper bore the names of such artists that he took seriously – Malevich, a nod to the Russian avant-garde; Van Gogh; Fra Angelico; and Massacio. On the third piece of paper was the name 'Leonardo da Vinci'. The following year Beuys repeated the same performance to great acclaim at the Zivilschutzräume in Basel, Switzerland.

In the month of May 1970 on his preliminary experience of the Moor of Rannoch, Richard Demarco introduced Joseph Beuys to The Road to Meikle Seggie via the Grampian Mountains. It was important that Joseph Beuys experienced the Celtic Kingdom of Dalriada on the shore of Loch Awe with 'its summer light of eternity'. Cutting a notch into a piece of bog pine, Beuys placed this in a lead box with a lump of peat and a Eurasian staff formed from copper, and an acknowledgement, 'What is it that gives you at its best the poetry associated with the Celts and the genius of St Columba whom Beuys regarded as one of the great revolutionary artists?

'Enduring and true art originates only in the meeting of friends.'

Before his untimely death in 1986, aged only 64, Joseph Beuys waas invited to experience Scotland on eight occasions.

Born in Capetown, South Africa, the educator and contemporary artist Jonathan Freemantle, whose work is represented in such worldwide collections as SABMiller, the Nirox Foundation and HM King Charles III, has also fallen under the spell of Demarco and Rannoch Moor.

'I first met Richard Demarco at Summerhall around 2012 and was instantly drawn to his magical aura,' he recalled. 'He has a glint in his eye, as if he is seeing beyond the ordinary and into a more illuminated strata of reality. At the time I was struggling to find my great subject, my *Golden Fleece*, and had decided to head into the Highlands in my old Mercedes in search of the "perfect mountain".

'Richard gave me four of his images of Joseph Beuys in an unmarked field and sent me off in search of this place. I returned to Edinburgh without finding this mysterious bog, but I did find my "perfect mountain".

'When I showed Richard the images of the mountain the glint in his eye sparkled even more mischievously. "It's the same place!" he said. I had found the great mountain Buachaille Etive Mòr, right next to Rannoch Moor, where he took Beuys in 1972.

'Something of the serendipity of this moment set the tone for our friendship. He has a genius that is rare. He is a great artist and a shaman. He has changed my life in so many ways.

'Being in Richard's presence is like entering into a world of heightened illumination, of wonder, excitement, romance. He carries with him an urgency bound together with love. He believes that things should be better and then shines his torch into the darkness so we may see how to make them better. He asks the right questions, questions that unlock the mystery.

'I am so grateful to have him in my life.'

16

Roaring stags

IN 1972 I KNEW THAT THE FUTURE OF THE EDINBURG FESTIVAL MUST INCLUDE THE GENUS OF KANTOR

IT SHOULD BE NOTED THAT THE KRZYSTOFORY CELLARS WERE USED BY TADEUSZ KANTOR TO PRESENT HIS AVANT GARDE CONCEPTS OF THEATRE E VISUAL ARTS DURING THE SECOND WORLD WAR

THE VISUAL AND THE PERFORMING ARTS WERE INTERTWINED BY TADEUSZ KANTOR!

I ALSO REALISED THAT IT HAD TO BE PART OF THE EDINBURGH FESTIVAL — ENTITLE "ATELIER 72" POLISH EXHIBITION

AS SOON AS I EXPERIENCED THIS MASTER PIECE I KNEW IT HAD TO BE PRESENTED AT THE 1972 EDINBURGH FESTIVAL

THERE IT WAS NOT EXPERIENCED IN A THEATRE BUT IN AN UNDERGROUND CELLAR DEEP BENEATH THE MEDIEVAL BUILDINGS IN CRACOW'S OLD TOWN

"THE WATERHEN" WAS WRITTEN AS A PLAY BY IGNACY WITKIEWICZ THIS WAS PRESENTED BY TADEUSZ KANTOR'S CRICOT TWO THEATRE COMPANY IT WAS PRESENTED IN THE KRZYSTOFORY GALLERY

I ENVISAGE THIS MANIFESTATION OF POLISH AVANT GARDE ART AS TAILOR MADE FOR THE RICHARD DEMARCO GALLERY'S FORREST HILL POORHOUSE AT ONE TIME A MEDIEVAL BEDLAM

The roaring stags of Glen Kinglas

THIS ARGYLLSHIRE FIEFDOM began in the first decade of the 20th century as the holiday dream of the Greenock-born physicist and armaments expert Sir Andrew Noble, latterly Chairman of Sir WG Armstrong, Whitworth & Co (later Vickers Armstrong) of Newcastle-upon-Tyne.

Having become significantly wealthy, Sir Andrew, by then well into his 70s, had previously holidayed in Argyll and locally in Cowal, and built on land owned from the 14th century by Clan Campbell. The existing Grade-A listed Ardkinglas House, which replaced two earlier mansion houses on the estate, was one of only four houses designed by the iconic Scots architect Sir Robert Lorimer, and represents a remarkable coupling of Edwardian wealth and artistic talent.

Situated at the landward end of Loch Fyne and just about an hour's drive from Glasgow via Loch Lomond, the waterfront setting could not be more spectacular, with extensive views across the water and south towards the hills of Kintyre. Sheltered by outstanding woodland and a landscape of remarkable beauty, it is today the home of Sir Andrew's great-great-grandson David Sumsion and his family.

Sir Andrew, who was made a Baronet in 1902, purchased the land in 1903 and the new house was completed in 1905. Lorimer, who fully grasped his client's urgent requirement for a romantic statement, used local granite and Caithness slate. Remarkable in its decorative detail inspired by the Art Nouveau and Scottish Arts & Crafts movement, all of the ornate fireplaces, light features, door handles and keyholes were personally supervised by the architect himself. Set into the windows of the pillared upper hall are stained-glass clan crests linking the Noble family to their romantic Scots ancestry.

After Sir Andrew's death aged 84 in 1915, summoned, according to local mythology by 'the roaring stags of Glen Kinglas,' his third son who was made a Baronet in his own right in 1923, made Ardkinglas his home. When he died in 1938, the estate was initially run by his two younger sons John and Michael, while Andrew, their elder brother, pursued a career in the British diplomatic service. Michael was later to distinguish himself as Secretary of State for Scotland in the Westminster Governments of Harold Macmillan and Sir Alec Douglas-Home and took the title of Lord Glenkinglas.

While John worked at Bletchley Park during the Second World

War, Ardkinglas was supervised by his wife Elizabeth as a home for evacuees from Glasgow following the Clydeside blitz. Post-war, John became active in promoting the arts in Scotland, becoming Chairman of both the Scottish Craft Centre and Edinburgh Tapestry Company. It was around this time that he and his wife Elizabeth inevitably came into contact with and became firm supporters of Richard Demarco and EDINBURGH ARTS.

Polish Cartography

As Marek Mutor of the Ossoliński National Institute was to discover on his visit to Falkland Palace, Poland's connections with Scotland stretch back far into the Middle Ages and were strongly enhanced in 1567 by a Royal Grant from King Stephen Báthory of Transylvania assigning a district of Krakow exclusively to Scottish immigrants. Scores of traders from Aberdeen and Dundee were to be found in Lviv, along with Scottish soldiers serving in the Polish Army.

The marriage of James Stuart, the Old Pretender, to Clementina Sobieska, a granddaughter of Jan Sobieski, King of Poland, was to some extent contrived to bring the Royal Houses of both countries closer together.

During the Second World War, the Polish Navy fought alongside the Royal Navy and the Polish Destroyer Squadron sought refuge in Leith, Rosyth, Port Glasgow, Greenock and Dundee. A plaque on a Polish Memorial in Prestwick commemorates the Polish sailors who died in the Battle of the Atlantic.

The majority of Polish soldiers stationed in the UK were quartered in Scotland, hence the noticeably large number who married the daughters of Scottish farmers and stayed behind. In 2013, Alan Beattie Herriot's bronze statue of Wojtek, the Syrian bear who became mascot of the Polish Artillery Supply Corps in the Italian Campaign, was erected in Edinburgh's Princes Street Gardens. Another statue was gifted by the Polish town of Zagan to Duns, in Berwickshire, with which it is twinned. Other statues of Wojtek can be seen in Cassino, Italy and Sopot in Pomerania.

Several Polish societies have been founded throughout Scotland and Edinburgh is twinned with the town of Krakow. Duns in Berwickshire is twinned with Zagan in the west of Poland. The Caledonian Society of Warsaw has recently commissioned the Royal kilt makers Kinloch Anderson in Leith to design a Warsaw tartan.

The conclusion of the Second World War brought unanimous joy to all concerned, but not to everybody. When the hostilities ended there were many Poles who had no desire to return to their homeland, among them Lieutenant General Stanisław Maczec who was stripped of his citizenship by the incoming Communist takeover.

Another such individual was the entrepreneurial Jan Tomasik, who had been a sergeant in the First Armoured Division quartered in Galashiels. Jan began his post-war career in Edinburgh washing floors with his wife Katarzyna and within three years saved enough money to buy and refurbish his own establishment, the first of many. Having discovered that his old wartime commander was living in poverty having been denied a war pension as a non-UK citizen, Tomasik employed him in various roles. Fortunately the Dutch Government also contributed a small pension in respect for his wartime service. In 1968, Tomasik bought the Black Barony Hotel on the outskirts of Peebles, and provided a holiday flat for his hero friend.

In 1989, the Polish Communist Prime Minister Mieczys Mieczysław Rakowski issued a formal public apology and in 1984 Maczec was awarded Poland's highest honour the Order of the White Eagle.

Lieutenant General Maczek died in 1994 at the age of 102. Whether it was under his influence or not, Tomasik employed Dr Kazimierz Trafas, a young cartographer from the Jagillonian University of Krakow, to design a vast horizontal concrete map, 40 x 50 metres, of Scotland, 'a gift to the Scottish people for the hospitality shown to the Poles during the war years.'

Although the Black Barony Hotel was sold in 1985, the map has been designated Historic Scotland Category B Listing in 2012 and lovingly repaired when necessary.

Bronisław Krzysztof's bronze statue of Lieutenant General Maczek seated on a bench can be seen in the quadrangle of Edinburgh's City Chambers.

Richard Demarco's relationship with Poland had begun as far back as 1963 when, as Director of The Traverse Gallery, he exhibited the work of Polish artists, and in 1966, organised a show entitled '40 Polish Film Posters'. The following year, at the newly established Demarco

Gallery in Melville Crescent, he presented an exhibition '15 Polish Artists', reciprocating with '15 British Artists' in Warsaw, visiting Warsaw to lay the foundations for an ongoing cultural exchange and dialogue.

Since then the romance with Poland has been constant. In 1972, the Demarco Gallery and Edinburgh International Festival collaborated on an unprecedented exhibition of Polish art entitled 'Atelier 72'. It featured Tadeusz Kantor, Magdalena Abakanowicz, Edward Krasinski, Natalia LL, Henryk Stażewski, Teresa Pągowska among others. The Poles are the classic Christo-Judaic dynamic of cultural heritage.

It seemed almost as if whenever the Scottish arts establishment turned its back on Richard Demarco, Poland threw open its creative arms to welcome him. There is even a Polish language publication of Richard Demarco essays edited by Krzysztof Noworyta.

At a reception held at the Black Barony Hotel in 1979, the Polish Ambassador Artur Starewicz awarded Richard Demarco with the Gold Medal of Merit on behalf of the Polish People's Republic.

17

Hebridean islands

LORD MACLEOD OF HUNTLY BECAME A STRONG SUPPORTER OF THE RICHARD DEMARCO GALLERY'S "EDINBURGH ARTS" PROGRAMMES LINKING THE EDINBURGH FESTIVAL'S HISTORY WITH THAT OF IONA. JEANNIE SANSHAGRAN AND THREE MEMBERS OF TADEUSZ KANTOR'S CRICOT TWO THEATRE COMPANY WERE PARTICIPANTS OF EDINBURGH ARTS 1976. THEY WERE JACEK STOKLOSA AND THE JANICKI TWINS

LORD MACLEOD OF FIUNARY AS FOUNDER OF THE IONA COMMUNITY LEADS 1976 EDINBURGH ARTS PARTICIPANTS ON THE SHORT VOYAGE FROM THE ISLAND OF MULL TO THE SACRED ISLAND OF IONA. AS MINISTER OF THE CHURCH OF SCOTLAND PARISH CHURCH IN GOVAN, SET ABOUT THE HEROIC TASK OF INSPIRING HIS PARISHIONERS TO RESTORE THE ANCIENT RUINS OF THE ABBEY FOUNDED BY SAINT COLUMBA ON IONA. LORD MACLEOD HAD MIRACULOUSLY SURVIVED THE TRENCH WARFARE OF THE FIRST WORLD WAR

Aboard *The Marques*

IN 1979, CHARLOTTE Doyle (later MacNair) signed up to administer EDINBURGH ARTS which that year took to the sea on board *The Marques*, the three-masted Spanish barque. 'We sailed from Cornwall to the Welsh coast and from there over to Southern Ireland and then across to Northern France,' she recalled happily.

'EDINBURGH ARTS was not just an opportunity to explore places and cultures, but involved a group of creative individuals journeying together and learning from each other. On *The Marques* it meant co-existing in a confined space at sea, washing in salt water and at some points feeling very seasick.

'Ricky liked to push people to their limits so that they could test themselves and those around them, and to work out their strengths and weaknesses. In doing so they produced interesting creative work from their experiences.

'Journeying with a constantly changing group of people was a fascinating concept and Ricky was extraordinary in how he coped with giving his time and energy to so many people, some of whom could be challenging and demanding. He was a teacher and liked to inspire and watch people grow – to get them to think differently. His enthusiasm knew no bounds and he never allowed obstacles to stand in his way.

'If Ricky had an idea or a vision, he had to make it work, not just talk about it. With people it was the same. Connecting people was an art form, and it taught me a great deal. People love to be introduced and learn from each other and to make lifelong friendships.

'*The Marques* experience was a formative one for many, most particularly for those who were on board as we sailed from Caldey Island off Wales to Kinsale in Southern Ireland,' she continued.

'That night there was a serious storm, which took lives in the Fastnet Race that was happening at the same time. We were lucky, but being at the mercy of the elements for many hours in total darkness with a black sea around us, was something I shall never forget.

'As dawn broke the storm abated and there was sudden light and calm, and Kinsale appeared out of the mist. John David Mooney from Chicago and I talk about this experience still after 45 years!

'EDINBURGH ARTS was an education for me in how to administer a complex project with people who all had different expectations and needs, but it allowed me to watch someone who was a master at making the world a magical place for those on that journey and showing them how important it was to grasp every opportunity a situation offered.

'Richard has an extraordinary talent. He did amuse, but he also shook people out of their "comfort zones" and allowed artists to cross boundaries and connect with people in order for them to understand each other and their respective worlds better.'

At a studio in Mallaig

Jon Schueler enlisted in the US Air Force shortly before America entered the Second World War in 1941, and thereafter served as a navigator on a B-17 Flying Fortress. When he was finally discharged on medical grounds he was one of only two survivors from its original crew. This impacted upon him for the rest of his life.

Suspended in the plane's plexiglass nose during the hazardous daylight raids over Germany and France, he developed his own highly complex relationship with the sky, one that would profoundly influence his art. He always claimed to have retained the 'angle of view from those flying days.'

When he set up a studio and painted at Mallaig in Morar on the west coast of Scotland, he got into the habit of going out in the fishing boats to find and draw inspiration from the coast and skies. He was quoted as saying, 'By going out to sea it detaches me from the ground. I'm in the painting, in the sky and the sea.'

Born in Milwaukee, Wisconsin, USA, Schueler was one of a second generation of brilliant American Abstract Expressionist painters, a group of whom by exhibiting in the Stable Gallery and Leo Castelli Gallery, established New York's place at the epicentre of the global art world in the 1950s, among them John Mitchell, Mark Rothko and Franz Kline. However, even when domiciled in New York, much of his career was dedicated to the exploration of nature.

Yet it was not until the end of the 1950s that he discovered Scotland, and from then on his painting techniques gradually changed. He abandoned the palate knife in favour of building up the paint in thinner layers applied to canvasses with large brushes. Throughout the 1960s, many of his paintings carried some vestige of the 'woman in the sky', hinting at the memory of his mother who had died when he was only six months old; later, sometimes, it was that of his wife Magda Salvesen, whom he first met at the Demarco Gallery in Melville Crescent where he held his first one-man Scottish exhibition. Magda had been working there on a voluntary basis and soon became his 'muse and companion'.

'I was working for the Demarco Gallery in Melville Crescent and interviewing the main artists that Ricky was showing or representing, putting together a dossier of up-to-date material and even interviews and photographs so that Ricky and the staff could quickly put together material for catalogues,' she recalled.

Encouraged by his friend the poet Alastair Reid, Schueler had come across Mallaig on his first visit to Scotland in 1957, a small fishing village on the Sound of Sleat. With horizon views of the islands of Eigg and Rum, and the southern tip of the Isle of Skye, he recalled that 'the geigercounter fell off the wall!'

'By the time of Jon's exhibition at the Demarco Gallery, I was working for the Scottish Arts Council as an Exhibition Officer, but I still have some material of Ricky's visit to Mallaig to see what the American was doing, from which came the invitation to show,' explained Magda.

'Also the paintings selected for the Demarco Gallery exhibition were all shown at the village hall in Mallaig and a wonderful crowd followed Ricky up to Mallaig for the opening. An amazing mixture of Mallaig people and incomers from Edinburgh!'

Richard reappeared in Mallaig a number of years later with his group on the sailing ship *The Marques*, which was moored in the harbour. 'They descended upon us in the pouring rain for lunch and then sailed away later over the sea to Skye!' She laughs at the memory.' It was surreal!'

Entranced by the distinctive northern light where the clouds were in perpetual motion, Schueler returned to New York and during the 1960s became an instructor at Yale University's Norfolk Summer School, then Head of Graduate and Undergraduate Painting and Sculpture at the University of Illinois at Urbana-Champaign.

In 1970, he returned to Mallaig to make it his home and occupy a studio in the former schoolhouse called Romasaig. This, he told his friends, became the backdrop for his dreams. Although admitting to having been to some extent influenced by JMW Turner and Clifford Still, his work firmly retained a unique and raw sensitivity, seeking out and capturing the light of truth or some deeper mystery.

Jon Schueler died in New York City in 1992, but his work continues to be exhibited throughout Scotland, America and Australia, supervised by his widow Magda who in 1999 wrote *The Sound of Sleat: A Painter's Life,* published by Picador USA.

Over the Sea to the Isle of Skye

If there was ever a man who fulfilled a dream, it was Sir Iain Noble Bt of Eilean Iarmain on the Isle of Skye. The eldest son of a British diplomat, Sir Andrew Noble, and the elder brother of John and Michael Noble of Ardkinglas. Iain was born in Berlin. At the time his mother was on a visit to her parents (her father was a Norwegian diplomat) who were stationed in the Norwegian Embassy. At the time his father was stationed in Rome, where he and his mother joined him and where he learned to walk on The Via Appia Antica.

Soon after this his father was appointed British Ambassador to China. When the Japanese army invaded China in 1937, Iain was imprisoned with his parents for nine months in a Shanghai hotel. When they were allowed to leave, in exchange for Japanese diplomats who had been imprisoned by the Allies, his father was posted to Buenos Aires and Iain was sent home to the United Kingdom to be educated. He did his National Service starting off with the Argyll & Sutherland Highlanders before transferring to the Intelligence Corps. His civilian career began with the insurance broker Matthews Wrightson & Co in London.

But commuting in London was an anathema to him and in 1968 he joined the Scottish Council (Development and Industry) in Edinburgh as a financial guru to develop theories and ideas as to how to strengthen Scotland's economy; in addition to look at innovative ways of addressing the problems of the Highlands and Islands where the rural communities were suffering. As the distinguished lawyer Sir Charles Fraser, Chairman of Lothian and Borders Enterprise, once observed, 'Iain had a bonnet full of ideas!'

At this time there was a very low morale in the Scottish business community and companies in Scotland were being bought over by large London-based conglomerates. Top management jobs were being lost and Iain maintained that if the trend continued, it would be disastrously detrimental to Scotland's long-term economy. He would often ask what Scotland's biggest export had been over three centuries? When the response came that it was anything from aggregates to Scotch Whisky, he would reply, 'No. Intellect!'

Another favourite quip was that every time a Scotsman crossed the Border into England, the IQ rose in both countries.

Iain had regularly discussed the potential of creating a Merchant Bank in Scotland with George Mathewson, Convenor of the Scottish Council (later Chairman of the Royal Bank of Scotland) who advised him to approach banking institutions in England. Iain's reaction was, 'If Scotland needs a merchant bank and no-one is prepared to do it, I'd better get on with it myself!'

Mythology has it that it was a conversation with Angus Grossart, a young Scots lawyer specialising in corporate tax law, while travelling on a bus to a National Trust for Scotland event, that led to the creation of Scotland's first independent Merchant Bank. Allegedly Angus was reluctant at first, protesting he was a lawyer not a banker, but Iain persisted. Thus Noble Grossart, Scotland's first Merchant Bank, came into being, operating initially from Iain's flat in Albyn Place where the Company Secretary answered the telephone calls seated on a stool in the hallway. In the aftermath of this, he founded over 20 different companies ranging from Shipping, Insurance and Oil (capitalising on the discovery of North Sea oil) to Scotch Whisky.

Iain had known his heart was in Scotland as a schoolboy. It was in Scotland that he wanted to live and work. When staying at the Noble family's home of Ardkinglas, where he was fostered by his Uncle John and Aunt Elizabeth, he would set off into the hills above Loch Fyne to absorb the names of the mountains and lochs where he soon became fluent in the Gaelic language through talking to the stalkers.

Deeply romantic by nature, Iain was in fact, deeply patriotic. Among his motivations was the preservation of Gaeldom's linguistic culture which he saw as an intrinsic part of the landscape. When in due course he sold his interest in Noble Grossart, he used the proceeds to buy the

23,000-acre Fearann Eilean Iarmain, the estate of Eilean Iarmain on Sleat and Strath, on the southern peninsula of the Isle of Skye.

Although not a born Gaelic speaker, Iain rapidly became fluent in the language and founded The Gaelic College Sabhal Mòr Ostaig in 1973. Today, Sabhal Mòr Ostaig is an academic partner of the University of the Highlands and Islands, and a multi-million-pound complex which, as an autonomous collegiate member, is unique in offering further education through the medium of Scottish Gaelic.

Iain was also responsible for the first dual-language road signs in Scotland and held the first Gaelic cheque book from the Bank of Scotland. Another of his initiatives was to conceive the Bicentennial Scotland Australia cairn built from stones collected from every parish in Scotland. Situated on the headland at Mossman, overlooking Sydney Harbour, this commemorates the landing of Captain Arthur Phillip in Australia in 1788 and Lachlan Macquarie, the 'Father of Australia' who was born of the Island of Ulva. As the Guest from Scotland of the Scottish Australian Heritage Council in 2006, Roddy Martine attended the annual cairn inspection ceremony where the name of Noble was regarded with much affection.

In 1979, Iain launched the Scotch Whisky company Pràban na Linne which produces the award-winning range of Gaelic whiskies, an enterprise which is continued by his widow Lucilla, whom he married in 1990. He was particularly proud that his whiskies, Poit Dhubh (Black Pot) and Te Bheag (Wee Dram) were unchilfiltered and he would say, 'Having Gaelic on the label greatly improves the flavour!'

Iain's friendship with Richard Demarco dated from the 1960s when Iain succeeded him as Deputy Chairman of the Traverse Theatre and he would loyally attend private views at the Demarco Gallery in Melville Crescent, notably those of Fleur Cowles and Patrick Heron. He also hosted memorable Burns Suppers at his Albyn Place flat. It was therefore inevitable that Demarco should have an exhibition at Eilean Iarmain in the early 1980s entitled 'The Search for the Celtic Soul'.

Roddy Martine also recalls visits to Eilean Iarmain; on one occasion to view the statues of Skye-based sculptor Laurence Broderick from Oxford. An especially fond memory was when he was researching his book *Supernatural Scotland* and Iain and his wife Lucilla took him up into the hills of the Sleat Peninsula to inspect a group of tiny 'Fairy Houses' that had been occupied centuries ago by The Small People.

'They became so small they eventually disappeared,' Iain explained with a straight face.

It was this warmth, curiosity and quiet humour that made him so special. However, it was his deeply embedded love for Scotland's artistic heritage in its widest international sense that made Sir Iain Noble Bt yet another national treasure, never to be forgotten.

On a visit to Sabhal Mòr Ostaig and Eilean Iarmain in May 2016, Richard inscribed the following in the Visitor's Book:

Here I am in the world of Iain and Lucilla and my mind is overcrowded with memories of how the Gaelic University came into being in the mind and heart of the human being who was born to fall in love with his soulmate who would help him make his dream come true and now exists as a unique and sacred place as a nodal point in the world of Gaelic culture.

I have a moral responsibility to focus on this point on the Island of Skye, where all aspects of Gaelic culture can flourish. I feel blessed to be here on this day so full of sunshine and high hopes for the future. I thank you Lucilla for the warmth of your welcome. As ever with love, Ricky.

Dhia a bhith maille ribh.

18

Ardfern, Inch Connell and Iona

The rocks remain

AFTER TWO- AND three-quarter centuries it is hard to imagine or exaggerate the bitter impact of the British Act of Proscription of 1746 which made virtually anything connected with Gaelic culture illegal. With the collapse of the Jacobite Cause on Culloden Moor there was simply no way that an Anglo/Lowland Protestant/Anglican government were going to encourage a Gaelic version of the *Book of Kells,* or the Scandinavian *Tales of Odin, Thor and Loki.*

Yet in 1765, when James Macpherson, a young Highland schoolmaster, claimed to have discovered the long lost poems of the bard Ossian, son of the Celtic warrior Fingal, miraculously preserved over 15 centuries, they became the *Harry Potter* sensation of the day.

Not only Scotland but Europe was taken by storm. Napoleon Bonapart took a copy of the book with him to Moscow and commissioned Jean-August Dominique Ingres to paint *The Dream of Ossian* for the ceiling of his bedroom in Rome. Thomas Jefferson wrote that he considered Macpherson to be the greatest poet that ever existed, and the composer Felix Mendelssohn was even inspired to write a symphony in admiration. The American essayist Henry David Thoreau compared the poems to Homer's *Iliad.*

Not so Dr Samuel Johnson who branded Macpherson a fraud.

So much debunking surrounds the epic of Ossian since the genius of James Macpherson either concocted or rescued Gaeldom's greatest work of romantic and oral legend, phoney or not. The jury is still out on their authenticity but they are an inspiring read. Meanwhile, Dr Samuel Johnson and the by then elderly Highland school teacher were both buried in Westminster Abbey.

You need to put it all into context. In the aftermath of three violent and pretty bloody Highland uprisings in support of the exiled Catholic Stuart 'Kings over the Water' in the late 17th and early 18th centuries, the last thing those in control wanted was a celebration of a heroic and glorious Caledonian twilight. Those primitive tribes of Dalriada (clans only emerged in the medieval age) were to be regarded as little more than heathen savages simmering in a cold climate. The concept of a mighty, noble race of romantic warriors was unacceptable; the idea of a fearless seafaring northern coastal and Hebridean civilisation was not to be either condoned or contemplated.

Nevertheless, such legends of Celtic, largely Irish, myth and the emergence of Dal Riata, not to mention the Knights Templar, proved fundamental to the revival of Scotland's self-awareness and self-confidence. William Shakespeare recognised this when trying to woo favour with James VI & I. Although foremost in the front rank of doubters, Sir Walter Scott recognised the potency of romantic fiction and he too shamelessly embraced the wonderment of immortality and days of yore.

In the western Highlands from which such tales emerge is Kilmartin Glen in Argyll containing one of the richest concentrations of prehistoric monuments and historic sites in Scotland. A circle of eight standing stones here have been dated from around 3000BC. The seductive mythology extends to the 80 sculpted stone grave slabs thought to be connected to the fugitive Templar Knights fleeing the greed of the King of France, and who created a workshop in the vicinity.

Occupied from the Iron Age, Dunadd is celebrated as the birthplace of Scotland, the capital of the long-ago kingdom of Dal Riata. On a flat outcrop of rock there is an incised carving of a boar in the Pictish style, an inscription in the ogham script from the eight century, and a footprint, all of which are thought to be integral to an ancient coronation ritual. In this extraordinary landscape, the past is ever present. Ossian, Fingal, Oscar and Malvina must surely have passed this way.

And it was on this glorious coastline following the traumatic night of Friday 13 1307, that a ship carrying fugitive Soldiers of Christ and of the Temple of Solomon, fleeing from Le Havre to escape a decree of excommunication imposed by Pope Clement V, landed its passengers. It was no accident. Since the recently proclaimed Scottish king, Robert the Bruce, embroiled in the war against King Edward of England, was under a similar order of excommunication, it was thought the Scots would welcome them with open arms. Seemingly they did, if there is any truth in the mysterious troop of knights in armour who arrived from nowhere to consolidate Bruce's victory at Bannockburn.

Writing in *Demarco 2020*, the film-maker Murray Grigor recalled, 'Ricky had already invited Mario and Marisa Merz (the only woman in the 'Arte Povera' movement who would later win the Biennale's major award, The Lion of Venice), to visit the Bronze Age landscape of the Kilmartin Valley on the west coast with its series of domed earth works. The next day we all set off on a traditional Demarco journey followed by our film crew. As we got out of our car, Ricky was already leading Mario and Marisa in their silver raincoats up the hill of Achnabreck. Although the sky was overcast their coats were shimmering in a ghostly light as they walked. When we caught up with them they were admiring an array of numerous concentric ring carvings on the exposed rock outcrop. As we began filming, Ricky turned to Mario, pointing to the many carved rings within rings on an outcrop of rock. "Look Mario, it's abstract art."

'As Mario studied the rock carvings rain began to spout tiny fountains over his silver coat. "The carvings on the rocks are the waves of raindrops hitting the water," replied Mario. "They are not abstract art!"

'Well,' Murray conceded, 'that was one great artist's theory on the enigma of the rings that have puzzled archaeologists and antiquarians for probably thousands of years. Although raindrops may not satisfactorily explain the one-metre-wide rings that are carved in the rock further up the glen!'

During the 1960s, Lunga House, a Victorian mansion at Ardfern, on the Craignish Peninsula, jutting out into the Atlantic between the Firth of Lorne and the Sound of Jura, became the West Coast outpost of the Demarco Gallery under the lairdship of the characterful, multitalented Colin Lindsay-MacDougall.

The story of the Lunga estate resonates through the centuries and the interplay between the vanquished Clan MacDougall and the ascendancy of Clan Campbell in the First War of Scottish Independence. Formerly known as Daill, the house originally belonged to the Campbells of Craignish until it was acquired in the 18th century by Colin's ancestor John, who took his Lunga designation from an island on the estate. Combining style with eccentricity, Lunga soon became a mecca for EDINBURGH ARTS. Colin fondly remembers how Richard Demarco and EDINBURGH ARTS touched the lives of a small Highland community in Argyll.

'Ricky's habit of artistic extemporisation reached a new peak when he requested board and lodging for about 25 Edinburgh Arts students, for a long weekend, at minimal cost, with negligible notice.

'Luckily, we had a Western Riding Week, just finishing, where a small marquee could be retained. Somehow, they were provided with basic Highland hospitality and became the start of a prolonged and wondrous adventure. Over succeeding years groups came by bus, ferry, or in convoys of kindly supporter's cars. Most memorably, they came in the magnificent square rigged sailing ship, *The Marques*.

'The journey became Art not just by expanding from the concept of The Road to Meikle Seggie, but by experiencing places and people which had direct connections to the land and even a journey as far back as the early Bronze Age temples, the innumerable Iron Age Brochs to the remote islands, where Celtic Christians created their understanding of religion and depicted it in stone.

'Together we contemplated the many sites with different forms of Cup and Ring marks, wondering if this was an early form of pictorial expression. This powerful shared experience was another form of visiting an artist's studio and it forged creative links and relationships which have endured into both the USA and Europe.

'As Ricky took Shakespeare's *Macbeth* out of the Proscenium Arch and brought it alive under screaming seagulls and wild stormy skies on the Island of Inchcolm, so EDINBURGH ARTS students sat on the grave of St Columba's mother, Queen Eithne, on the remote Garvellach Islands. In so doing, they were passing from the almost complete early Christian beehive dwellings to the similar partially ruined homes of the slate workers who had re-roofed St Petersburg after it was burned in the Napoleonic Wars.

'Walking and talking in a quiet glen, shrouded in soft West Highland mist, with such as Günther Uecker, Joseph Beuys or Marion Calder. Ideas were flowing. Sharing a picnic, waves lapping on the shore, with Arthur Sackler who was explaining the finer details of connoisseurship. This is only a hint of the special experiences which formed part of the journey.

'The Duchess of Argyll led a lucky group up a secret track to the Moon Pool, high above Inveraray Castle, where, on a hot afternoon, they could swim naked and rest to hear the stories of the tower called Dun na Cuaiche, on the neighbouring peak. It had been built during the Little Wars of Lorne, to ensure that a watcher could warn and ensure that no MacDonalds could creep up on the Campbell stronghold, as Colkitto did in 1644.

'Being on such a spectacular peak, it became a tiny point of focus for the invasion of Normandy in the Second World War. The crack troops destined to lead the way up the beaches trained at Inveraray and had to run to this tower, each morning before breakfast to sign the book.

'So many tales, so many special experiences, so many discovered places. Maybe it is this unique form of Art, so special to Scotland, that enables Richard Demarco to touch all of our lives.'

In the footsteps of St Columba

South-west and off the coast of the rain washed, windswept and midge rampant island of Mull in the Scottish Inner Hebrides lies the tiny sacred island of Iona. It was here in 563AD that the Irish monk Saint Columba stepped ashore on the island's white sandy beaches with his 12 followers in tow to found the Christian community which lasts to this day.

For over a millennium, Iona has survived as a beacon of ecumenical light on the western shores of Europe. For Scotland, it has had the added distinction of being the burial ground of 48 kings of Dalriada (Pictland/Scotland), eight Norwegian and five Irish kings, including Kenneth 1 of Scotland (MacAlpin) and Macbeth. They have been joined here by countless chiefs of Clan Donald, Maclean and Macleod.

As the Celtic church began to lose momentum and gave way to the Church of Rome, a nunnery was established for Black Nuns in 1203, followed by a Benedictine Abbey. To begin with there were fierce Viking attacks to contend with, then along came the Reformation four centuries later. After that, everything more or less fell apart until 1899 when ownership of the island and ruined Abbey and Nunnery was transferred from the eighth Duke of Argyll to the Iona Cathedral Trust.

A general restoration began but progressed slowly into the 20th century being interrupted by the First World War. Cometh the moment, cometh the man, and that man was the towering figure of the Reverend George MacLeod, a former soldier, heir to a Scottish baronetcy and also a grandson of the Scottish Manse.

Having been ordained into the Church of Scotland in 1924, MacLeod was deeply affected by the politics of the day. Becoming increasingly concerned with social inequality and the growing unemployment of the 1930s, he went on to found the Iona Community in 1938, determined to rebuild the abbey as the centre of a thriving international ecumenical settlement. The Iona Community had, and still retains, four purposes:

mission, political involvement, a ministry for healing, and the facility for worship. Over the following years, it steadily matured into a force to be reckoned with through adopting a worldwide constitution for the Federation of Earth, and as such, it continues to work for justice and peace, the rebuilding of communities and the renewal of worship.

So thus it was here on 8 August 1980 that the rented Spanish barque *The Marques,* as the replica of Charles Darwin's HMS *Beagle,* arrived from the Scottish mainland. On board with Richard Demarco and his contingent crew of EDINBURGH ARTS was the Gaelic poet Sorley MacLean. They were welcomed by the (by then ennobled) Lord MacLeod of Fuinary in person.

George Macleod's son Maxwell, a keen supporter of Richard and EDINBURGH ARTS from a young age, was also on board. 'It's a cliché I know, but one of Ricky's trips changed my life,' he recalled. 'We had tasted savagery and found it didn't work. We did art and became more civilised! I still dream of *The Marques.* And one of the cooks.'

Appendix

RICHARD DEMARCO

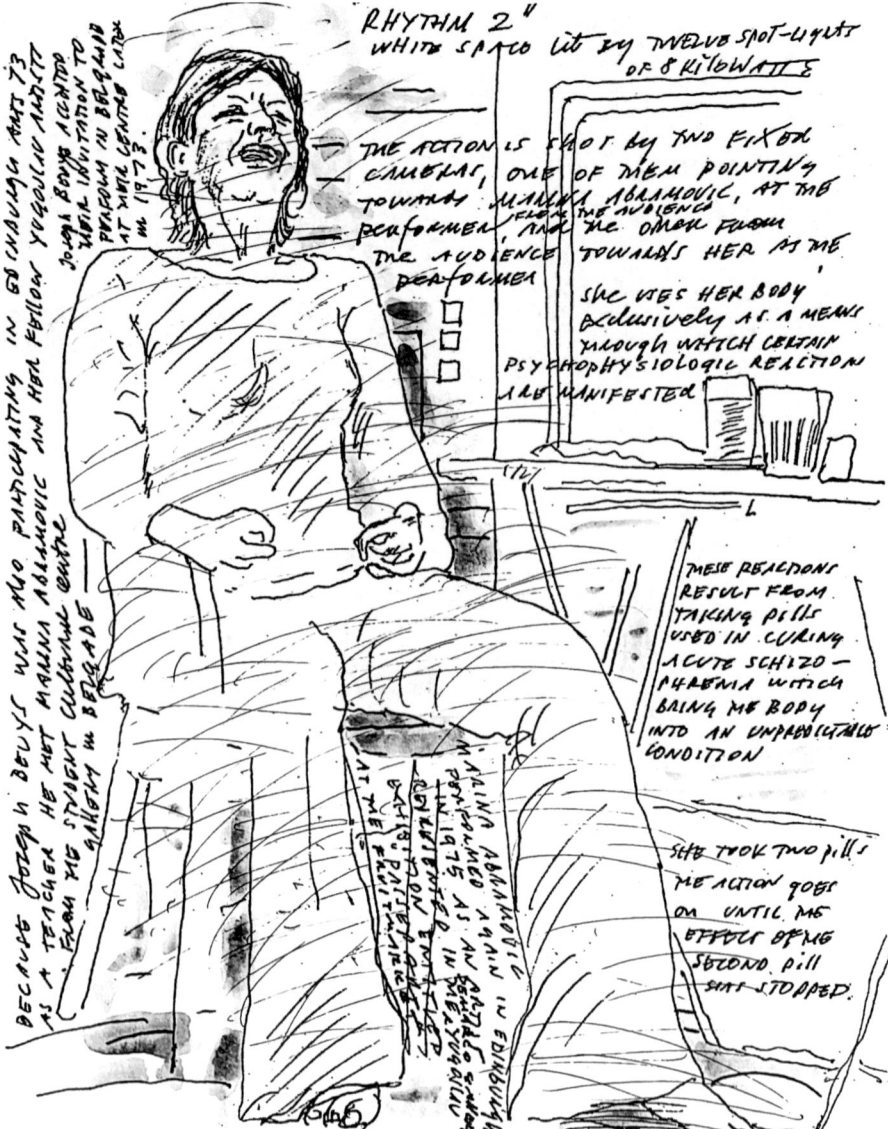

RHYTHM 2"
WHITE SPACE lit by TWELVE SPOT-LIGHTS OF 8 KILOWATTS

THE ACTION IS SHOT BY TWO FIXED CAMERAS, ONE OF THEM POINTING TOWARDS MARINA ABRAMOVIC, AT THE PERFORMER FROM THE AUDIENCE AND THE OTHER FROM THE AUDIENCE TOWARDS HER AS THE PERFORMER

SHE USES HER BODY EXCLUSIVELY AS A MEANS THROUGH WHICH CERTAIN PSYCHOPHYSIOLOGIC REACTION ARE MANIFESTED

THESE REACTIONS RESULT FROM TAKING PILLS USED IN CURING ACUTE SCHIZO-PHRENIA WHICH BRING THE BODY INTO AN UNPREDICTABLE CONDITION

SHE TOOK TWO PILLS THE ACTION GOES ON UNTIL THE EFFECT OF THE SECOND PILL HAS STOPPED.

BECAUSE JOSEPH BEUYS WAS ALSO PARTICIPATING IN EDINBURGH ARTS 73 AS A TEACHER HE MET MARINA ABRAMOVIC AND HER FELLOW YUGOSLAV ARTISTS FROM THE STRAIGHT CURRENT CENTRE GALLERY IN BELGRADE

JOSEPH BEUYS ACCEPTED THEIR INVITATION TO PERFORM IN BELGRADE AT THE CENTRE LATER IN 1973

MARINA ABRAMOVIC PERFORMED RHYTHM 2 IN EDINBURGH IN 1975 AS AN EDINBURGH EXHIBITION OF YUGOSLAVIA ... COMPLETED TOTALLY DIFFERENT EXHIBITION OF RHYTHM 2 AT THE FRUITMARKET GALLERY

MARINA ABRAMOVIC FIRST PRESENTED HERSELF AS A PERFORMANCE ARTIST AS A PARTICIPANT ON EDINBURGH ARTS 1973 — PERFORMING AT MELVILLE COLLEGE IN AUGUST AS PART OF MY DEMARCO GALLERY'S YUGOSLAV DIMENSION IN ITS VISUAL ARTS PROGRAMME SHE WAS THE ARTIST HONOURED BY THE FRUITMARKET GALLERY WITH THEIR 1995 EDINBURGH FESTIVAL EXHIBITION

Of Vocation and Language

THE NODAL POINTS on my life's journey have depended almost entirely on how I have shared my firm belief that the spirit of the Edinburgh Festival should not be restricted to a period of three weeks during what, in Scottish history, is known as The Lamas Tide. That is the time of late summer dominated by the harvesting of nature's plenitude.

These nodal points came into being over a period of time, linking the decades of the '50s, '60s and '70s. I do believe that my friendships with key fellow explorers of what I have come to entitle 'The Road to Meikle Seggie' remain vital to the way I deal with experiencing the third decade of the Third Millennium.

I am indebted to Gavin MacDougall for enabling me to conjoin my memories of the Edinburgh Festival with those of Roddy Martine who has suggested, in a recent telephone conversation with me, that *Demarco's Scotland* should be focused on the challenge I face in having to cope with an overload of memories of the Edinburgh International Festival as a nonagenarian. He suggests I should concentrate on what I consider is my future and, therefore, on what I suppose could be considered as the legacy I have left involving those creative friends with whom I have been fortunate to collaborate throughout my 94th year.

I can consider that I have been particularly blessed by all those who enabled me to consider the immediate future and, therefore, the challenge of this year's period dedicated to what is defined as the period of the Edinburgh International Festival. The Demarco Gallery's experiment in education on a tertiary level extended the period of the Edinburgh International Festival up to eight weeks, beginning with the Summer Solstice and ending in mid-September. The programme that I am slowly but surely envisioning will be defined by a combination of symposia and the physical experience of exploring The Road to Meikle Seggie, knowing that this Road is inevitably pointed in the direction of the Continent of Europe.

The programme of symposia will be focused on that vitally important aspect of the Demarco Archive expressed in the photographic medium; that is, in a combination of film, video, publication and what is now regarded as a completely new genre of contemporary art expressed in what is defined as Event Photography.

Over the period of the recent past, I have been presented with a multitude of unexpected challenges. These have caused me to bring thoroughly up-to-date what I consider to be the future of the Demarco Archive, not as an archive but as a gigantic and challenging total art work and as an unique form of academic resource focused on history, art history, philosophy and religion under the aegis of a university school of humanities.

On the 50th anniversary of the Edinburgh International Festival, Edinburgh University invited the distinguished scholar, Professor George Steiner, to deliver a lecture in Edinburgh University's McEwan Hall. George Steiner made it clear in this lecture that the worlds of culture and education are but two sides of the same coin. I know that I have always endeavoured to take this truth into consideration and it now seems inevitable that, in 1972, the Demarco Gallery's raison d'etre became a university of all the arts.

As such, it involved the art of Joseph Beuys who declared to me that his art was essentially resulting from his self-appointed task as a teacher using what he defined as 'social sculpture'. As an expression of his mindset, he rejected the safety of the major museum, the Fridericianum, coveted museum space at the heart of the concept of dOCUMENTA. In doing so, he concentrated on artistic spirit upon the threat of global warming by an art work which questioned the role of the artist in contemporary society. He suggested that social sculpture was literally about re-shaping the very nature of society and gave to the artist of the Third Millennium the role of combating the threat of global warming.

I am, therefore, obliged to envision my programme for this year's Edinburgh Festival to begin in the journeys towards Edinburgh. Two of these have already become a reality. One, led by a long-term artist friend Fenya Starkey from the south coast of England at Eastbourne via the world of Saint Columba at Durham Cathedral and on Holy Island, and the other led by Io Worthington, a young graduate of Glasgow School of Art, from London via the Inner Hebrides and Rannoch Moor.

There have also been explorations of the ancient pilgrimage routes as well as those of medieval scholars beginning in Scotland and completing them in such universities as The Sorbonne.

I am well aware that my life as an artist-teacher has benefited from the honorary degrees conferred on me by Stirling, Dundee, Leeds

Beckett, Solent and Atlanta, Edinburgh and Wrocław universities. I wish to make good use of my involvement in the world of academe on three levels of education – primary, secondary and tertiary.

I feel I must emphasise the fact that I was fortunate, through the decade of the '90s, to be Kingston University's Professor of European Cultural Studies under the patronage of Professor David Youlton. I am thinking of the ways in which I have been inspired by universities throughout the world and the treasure house of their libraries.

For me, the history of Scotland is not just to be found in the National Library of Scotland but in the libraries of historic houses such as Traquair, Fingask, Ledlanet, Marchmont, Elsieshields, Dalkeith, Hopetoun, Bemersyde, Mellerstain, Lunga and Falkland, as well as the Signet Library of Scotland. I have identified all of these houses with manifestations of my cultural and academic contributions to the history of the Edinburgh Festival and the best example would be the Highland Shakespeare Company of which I have the honour to be associated with as its patron.

Of course, I have always considered that Scotland's history and its culture is distinctly entwined with the history of Europe and the Edinburgh International Festival. It therefore helped to establish this fact into the history of the 20th century and inevitably into the Third Millennium. I do believe that my collaboration with Joseph Beuys helped identify the Demarco Archive with the Beuysian concept of '7,000 oaks' as a statement possessed of a cultural and political significance in the battle now being fought by humankind against the threat of global warming.

This is the land where, in the entire world of Nature in the United Kingdom, you can find a well-nigh perfect world of academe with innumerable trees, the close proximity of a mountain-scape, innumerable species of animals, plants and insects and panoramic landscapes where history and mythology intertwine, as well as a colony of red squirrels and the rushing waters over a Highland river. This should not be the stuff and substance of a dreamscape. In fact it is a reality and it does exist in the world of Glenalmond College with its emphasis on outdoor education.

Recently, I experienced the opposite of an urban academic landscape when I attended two graduation ceremonies – the first on the campus of Stirling University and two days later, at the graduation ceremony on the campus of Glenalmond College. They are both located within two Scottish mountainous landscapes, each of 330 acres. Together on primary, secondary and tertiary levels of academe, they represent the ideal world of education in which the natural world is dominant.

Like Joseph Beuys, I am possessed of a vocation as a teacher and that is why I invited him, as the co-founder of Green politics in Germany, to place the language of all the arts at the forefront of education.

It was on the Argyllshire hills surrounding Loch Awe that Joseph Beuys was first inspired to create his sculptural masterpiece entitled '7,000 Oaks' as an expression of his concept of 'social sculpture'.

I therefore think it is appropriate to end this essay by quoting a text from my interview with him in Brooks Club in London in 1982 as he prepared himself for the seventh dOCUMENTA exhibition in Kassel.

RICHARD DEMARCO: I would like you to tell me how you can see a link between the present exhibition and this next step that you will take, this major work involving the planting of seven thousand oak trees at the dOCUMENTA in Kassel. You see it as a natural and inevitable step linking the world of the artist with that of the ecologist and naturalist. You will concentrate all your energy on this and I would like you just to comment on this and in some way relate to this as a sculpture, involving very powerfully from my viewpoint, the dimension of time.

JOSEPH BEUYS: It is right, and you see already in this title the words 'last space' appear in relation to time. This is not as a demise for my doings. It puts a kind of line under my so-called spatial doings in so-called environments. I wanted principally to mark the finish of this kind of work. I wish to go more and more outside to be among the problems of nature and problems of human beings in their working places. This will be a regenerative activity; it will be a therapy for all of the problems we are standing before... That is my general aim. I proposed this to Rudi Fuchs when he invited me to participate in the dOCUMENTA. I said that I would not like to go again inside the buildings to participate in the setting up of so-called artworks. I wished to go completely outside and to make a symbolic start for my enterprise of regenerating the life of humandkind within the body of society and prepare a positive future in this context.

Reflections on the 50th anniversary of EDINBURGH ARTS

My first thoughts on the actual structure of the programme that I envision for EDINBURGH ARTS 2024 on the 50th anniversary of the EDINBURGH ARTS 1974, when I presented the now historic 'Black and White Oil Conference', questioning the political decision to commit the economic future of Scotland to the birth of North Sea oil as a non-renewable energy resource.

EDINBURGH ARTS 74 had become historic also because it committed itself to supporting the need for penal reform in Scotland by supporting the Special Unit in Glasgow's HMP Barlinnie. This involved me inviting Jimmy Boyle as an artist and inmate of the Special Unit, to spend his first and only day of freedom from his life imprisonment in the world of EDINBURGH ARTS in which I could arrange for him to meet Joseph Beuys, arguably the world's most controversial and highly respected artist.

This year will also mark 50th anniversary of the friendship between Jimmy Boyle and Helen Crummy. This resulted in Jimmy Boyle being invited to create a large-scale prone figure in concrete of Jonathan Swift's 'Gulliver'.

EDINBURGH ARTS enabled the Demarco Gallery to be deeply involved in the most pressing problems within the structure of Scottish society. It invited artists, art teachers and their art students to face the challenge in the 1970s of much-needed penal reform in Scotland. It also questioned the role of the artist under the aegis of the official Edinburgh Festival programme at a time when Joseph Beuys co-created green politics in Germany.

EDINBURGH ARTS 2024 will focus on the political issues facing Scotland as a European country dealing with the threat of European democracy in the tragic reality of the war being fought on the Russian–Ukrainian border. This year's EDINBURGH ARTS programme will, therefore, cover a period of three weeks, beginning in mid-July and ending in a week-long period during the three weeks of the official programme of the Edinburgh Festival.

This two-week programme will begin in Scotland in the historic Peeblesshire world of Traquair House. It will provide the starting point of what I know as 'The Road to Meikle Seggie', following in the footsteps of Joseph Beuys and of a number of his fellow Düsseldorf artists who took part in the 1970 Richard Demarco Gallery exhibition with the palindromic title 'Strategy: Get Arts'. These artists were the painter Gerhard Richter, the sculptor Günther Uecker, the composer Friedhelm Döhl, and the film-maker Lutz Mommartz. They all considered The Road to Meikle Seggie as 'The Road to the Isles' with the particular destination in the form of the studio of Jon Schueler, the American painter inspired by the skies above the Sound of Sleat, separating the fishing port of Mallaig from the mountainous Isle of Skye and the world where Sir Iain Noble had established the Gaelic College at Sabhal Mòr Ostaig.

I am indebted to Michael Lloyd for undertaking the concept of a 'cinema' in the historic setting of Dalkeith Palace, in close collaboration with Charlotte Rostek who is leading the development of Dalkeith Palace. The period of 21 days in July will focus on what I consider as nodal points on The Road to Meikle Seggie. They will, of course, take into account the 1974 Demarco Gallery housed within the walls of what was Edinburgh University's Forrest Hill Poorhouse abutting the church and graveyard of Greyfriars in the very heart of Edinburgh's medieval city, beneath the battlements of Edinburgh Castle.

Among those EDINBURGH ARTS veterans who took part in the early programmes are those who will be invited to speak of their personal memories in a programme of conferences, masterclasses and symposia. Among them will be Jane MacAllister, Charles Stephens, David Petherick, Jane Chisholm, Gabriella Cardazzo, Colin Lindsay-MacDougall, Clare Adams, Anne Goring, John Armstrong, Sandy Nairne, Mark Francis, Sally Potter, Jacky Lansley, Zbigniew Makarewicz, Caroline Tisdall, Richard England, Sue Finlay, Timothy Emlyn Jones, Tina Brown, Jenny Agutter, Helen Mirren, Peter Selz, Marina Abramović, Stuart Hopps, Jennifer Gough-Cooper, Pippa Drysdale, John David Mooney, Neill Slaughter, Bill Beech and Jane Whitaker. These talks would also include reference, from the Demarco Archive, to Hugh MacDiarmid, Patrick Reyntiens, George Wyllie, Dawson Murray, Jim Haynes, Sir Roland Penrose, Ian Hamilton Finlay, Paul Neagu, Horia Bernea, Stanisław Ignaci Wietkiewicz, Henryk Staszewski, Jerzy Nowosielski, Tadeusz Kantor, Zofia Kalińska, Maria Stangret, Jack Tworkov, Tom Hudson, Magdalena Abakanowicz, Basil Skinner and Bogusław Schaeffer. They were all introduced to the world of Edinburgh's Dean, Duddingston and

Cramond villages; the prehistoric hill fort of Arthur's Seat; Helen Crummy's Craigmillar Festival; Peter and Flora Maxwell Stuart's Traquair House; the estates of Dalmeny and Hopetoun on the shorelines of the Firth of Forth; Holyrood Abbey and Palace and the castles of Craigmillar and Lauriston, Rosslyn Chapel, Castle and Glen; Sue and Ian Hamilton Finlay's Stonypath Farm in Lanarkshire, which became world-famous as the sculptural garden of 'Little Sparta'; and in the Scottish Borders, the houses and estates of Abbotsford, Arniston, Bemersyde, Marchmont, Mellerstain and Drumlanrig; the Border Abbeys of Melrose, Dryburgh and Kelso, and, of course, in the Kingdom of Fife, Ledlanet House and estates; Meikle Seggie as a working farm in the foothills of the Ochil Hills; the Palace of Falkland and Dunfermline Abbey and St Andrews Castle and University. It also included the world of St Columba on Iona in Argyllshire in the Celtic Kingdom of Dalriada, particularly in the Valley of Kilmartin, the house and estates of Lunga and Inverary Castle.

Today, I had a most inspiring meeting with Angie Cairns and Alexandra Mathie. They have spent their formidable creative energies over many years on Scotland's outstanding women artists. They have planned meetings today in Edinburgh with Scotland's National Galleries and with Lyon & Turnbull auction house. They are wholeheartedly in agreement with Terry Ann Newman and myself that it is only a rumour that such artists as Joan Eardley, Margot Sandeman and Patricia Douthwaite are no longer alive. (This year marks the 90th anniversary of Patricia Douthwaite's birth.)

I have to plan a symposium on their contribution to the cultural life of Scotland. Of course, I must also pay homage to other artists who have recently died, such as Dawson Murray, Phillip Bruno, Hugo Burge, Camilla Raemaekers, John Cairney, Lesley Main, Ian Hunter, Magdalena Abakanowicz, Ainslie Yule, Dorothée Bouchard and Giuliano Gori.

The EDINBURGH ARTS programme 2024 will explore The Road to Meikle Seggie and those nodal points which identify this Road as the drovers' roads of Europe and those travelled by medieval pilgrims and scholars and those EDINBURGH ARTS participants who were prepared to follow it as far as the Apennine Mountains linking Rome with Naples from where my Demarco ancestors lived their lives as farmers and as shepherds, not only during the Roman Empire but further back in time to pre-history. It is the Road which binds the Demarco Archive to that of the Ossolineum Institute in the Polish City of Wrocław, focused on the fact that the second language of Scotland is now Polish resulting from the years of the Second World War during which the Polish Army trained in Scotland to fight with courage under the Generals Anders and Maczek. The Yalta Conference resulted in the heroic Polish soldiers being betrayed so that they could not return to their beloved homeland which was then under the brutal Government of Stalinist Communism.

The Polish Army have made their presence felt, even to this day, in the Scottish Borders and the Kingdom of Fife, particularly in the Palaces of Dalkeith and Falkland, and the historic castle of Black Barony and the houses and estates of Marchmont and Traquair.

I am conscious that my contribution to what I must identify as an 'alternative' Edinburgh Festival will be in no way aligned to the official or Fringe Festivals' programmes. The Demarco Archive is essentially an authentic academic resource and, sadly, neither the Fringe nor the official Festival will offer academic information.

I was much impressed by the lecture at Robert McDowell's Summerhall Arts Centre given by Mella Shaw; it gave me hope for the future of the present-day art world. She entitled her exhibition 'Sounding Line', resulting from the fact that she has been concerned by the plight of countless whales beached on the shores of the Outer Hebrides.

Her art is inspired by how our modern world is interfering with the capacity of whales to navigate the oceans of the world due to the overcrowded nature of world shipping, causing sonic pollution. Mella Shaw has confronted a major problem facing humanity's relationship with the natural world. She embodies the legacy of Joseph Beuys, binding together the worlds of art and science.

The Demarco Archive: a unique manifestation of art language

THIS BOOK PROVIDES proof that the Demarco Archive traces the history and explores beyond Edinburgh's civic boundaries into the reality of Scotland's inspiring landscape revealed by the signposts on what I have described as 'The Road to Meikle Seggie'.

Both *Demarco's Edinburgh* and *Demarco's Scotland* are inspired by what I believe is a unique manifestation of the Demarco Archive, NOT as an archive and not even as an exhibition but as a total art work in the ideal environment, not as an art gallery but as a historic library. However, the Signet Library is a work of art in itself. It can be described as a thing of architectural beauty. It came into being inspired by Sir Walter Scott. It expresses the spirit of the Scottish Enlightenment in the way it thus aspires to the condition of sculpture.

During the Edinburgh Festival 2022, it provided me with the perfect location to celebrate the entire history of the Edinburgh Festival. Now, to mark my 94th birthday in July this year, I feel it is my moral responsibility to bring the Demarco Archive thoroughly up to date.

In 1947, the Edinburgh International Festival was undoubtedly a healing balm in the aftermath of World War Two. Now, the Edinburgh Festival must provide proof that the language of all the arts can heal the wounds now threatening humanity from global warming and human conflict, and can, in 2024, reveal the 'flowering of the human spirit'.

This year's Edinburgh Festival must express my deep gratitude for the gift I have received of a long life. Also, I need to express my gratitude to all my fellow artists and personal friends as well as my family living and dead. I do earnestly believe that true art originates in the meetings of friends, particularly if they are provided with the opportunity to become 'artist explorers' on what I have come to identify as The Road to Meikle Seggie, that is the road to the world of nature, particularly those of farmscapes.

Now, mankind has the power to develop industrial farming. This is clearly not the way in which we should deal with Mother Nature. The surface of the earth must be treated with gentle and loving care. The small farmer such as the Scottish crofter must be regarded with respect.

The members of the EDINBURGH ARTS faculty and their students began their academic studies by exploring the world of the farmers in the Ochil Hills lying between the Kingdom of Fife and the hillscapes of Perthshire, the domain of Shakespeare's *Macbeth* and his three witches between the oak trees of Birnam and Dunsinane.

The artist, therefore, should avoid making art for the art world – and acknowledge art as the language which is most effective in dealing with today's world beset by false truths and the language of the propagandist. The artist's role is to be likened to that of the Ukrainian soldier fighting in the trenches of the front line against Russian autocracy; that is, fighting for the spirit of democracy.

I have always believed that the serious artist is well-equipped to fight against those who would rely on the language of the politician, the banker, the lawyer, the accountant whose lives, in the main, are shorn of the compassion and even love for those suffering from a social structure that causes the rich to become richer and the poor to become poorer.

I have just been asked to make the final address to those attending the two-day conference presented by the European Movement in Scotland. It took place in Robert McDowell's Summerhall Arts Centre. I illustrated my address with the map I had drawn in the Millennium year of 2000. This map provided proof that I have never managed to live within the confines of the British Isles. I have always operated inspired by the Edinburgh Festival with the firm belief that Scotland, by its very history and language, was a vital part of the European Continent and that, indeed, long before the British Empire existed, the Antonine Wall defined the North-Western extremity of an empire which linked the banks of the Rivers Forth and Clyde with the shorelines of The Baltic, Mediterranean, Adriatic and Black Seas.

I explained that this map provided proof that the blood that courses through my veins is of a Romano-Celtic mixture. The name on my birth certificate is Riccardo Demarco and is clearly associated with Europe.

However, I must never forget that the Celts and the Romans came from the Mediterranean and, indeed, the Celts were not from Northern Europe. They came from the coastline of what is now identified as that of Palestine and Gaza. There is an old legend which says that the Irish were the Jews of long ago and that the 13th tribe of Israel is that of the Irish. The founding director of the Edinburgh Festival was Rudolph Bing, an Austrian and also Jewish and thoroughly European.

He and his friends gifted the concept of the Edinburgh International Festival so that Edinburgh became not only the capital of Scotland but more significantly the world capital of culture.

The European Youth Parliament will celebrate its 100th anniversary in Greece this year. All my EDINBURGH ARTS expeditions were focused on the mysterious ways in which the islands of the Cyclades are linked to those of the Hebrides and that the great god Apollo flies like an eagle from Delphi to that part of Europe beyond where the North Wind blows.

Sir William Gillies Lecture, The Royal Scottish Academy 2010

In the year 2010, the Royal Scottish Academy celebrated my 80th birthday by presenting an exhibition curated by Arthur Watson as the Academy's President, together with Euan MacArthur, the art historian and colleague at Dundee University's Duncan of Jordanstone College of Art and Design.

They gratefully received financial support from the Ministries of Culture of Poland, Romania, Germany, Serbia and from Creative Scotland as well as from the British Council, in order to present the Academy's exhibition entitled 'Ten Dialogues – Richard Demarco and the European Avant-garde'.

I was invited to deliver the Academy's Sir William Gillies Lecture on 25 November 2010 in the National Galleries of Scotland's Hawthornden Lecture Theatre. I carefully wrote a nine-page text entitled 'The Challenge of the New Europe' as an updated version of The Stanley Picker Lecture I gave in 1992 as a Kingston Polytechnic Stanley Picker Fellow.

I seem to be wearing the hat that I last wore at The Royal Academy's Burlington House in 1993 in giving my first professorial address as Kingston University's Professor of European Cultural Studies. Under the title 'The Challenge of the New Europe', I spoke of the role that Britain must take in relation to the 11 countries which constituted then the European Union. Much has changed in the last two decades and, now, there are 27 European member states to consider, all of which are in relation to the title which the Royal Scottish Academy has given to the exhibition 'Ten Dialogues: Richard Demarco, Scotland and the European Avant-garde'.

In 1993, I was heading towards playing the game of life in my 70s, that is, 'in extra time' and now I am speaking to you playing the game of life in my 80s 'in penalty shoot-out time', facing challenges the likes of which I have not known in my adult life. I know that there are a few fellow octogenarians in this lecture theatre. I rely on them to verify the many facts which I have to take into account over the past six decades.

The slide projector is my preferred way of illustrating my lectures. It is a method which will soon become obsolete in this computerised age. Many of these slides symbolise a journey over land and sea on what I have come to define as The Road to Meikle Seggie. This journey echoed that made by Sir Roland Penrose, the very personification of the artist who played the role of art patron, particularly through his direction of the Institute of Contemporary Arts in Dover Street. He was a good friend of David Baxandall, the Director of the National Galleries of Scotland. They both gave vitally important support to the Demarco Gallery in the first year of its existence.

Roland Penrose made a historic journey in 1938 together with his wife, Lee Miller. They drove her classic Packhard from Athens through the primitive highways and byways of Bulgaria and Romania towards Bucharest. These roads are now modernised but the landscape still holds a unique enchantment, unmistakably recognisable as Meikle Seggie heartland. Their adventures are expressed in a book illustrated by the drawings and paintings of Roland Penrose and the photographs of Lee Miller. This book is in a limited edition, a treasured part of the Demarco Archive. It is entitled *The Road is Wider than Long*. It could well define the quintessential nature of The Road to Meikle Seggie.

My slides are at the heart of the Demarco Archive. The majority of these bring back vivid memories for me because I was responsible for taking the vast majority of the photographs. However, I must make it clear that I do not regard myself as a photographer and as proof of that I am grateful to the Museum Kunst Palast in Düsseldorf and the team of archivists under the direction of Stephan von Wiese.

They have focused their attention upon identifying a new genre of modern art. It is entitled 'Event Photography'. They have referred to me as an exponent of this genre. I was thus invited to attend the exhibition opening and give a lecture illustrated by my event photography. The artists involved all used the camera but they were identified, not as photographers, but as artists in meaningful collaboration with artists. The resultant photographic images provided proof positive that such collaborations added a necessary new dimension to such artists as Gerhard Richter, Günther Uecker, Joseph Beuys, Blinky Palermo, Leon Tarasewicz and Joanna Przybyla.

It should be noted that a significant number of my slides are perfect examples of 'event photography', particularly those relating to the ten artists who have been selected to make manifest the Royal Scottish Academy exhibition related to this William Gillies Lecture.

It should also be noted that the first slide, showing the physical reality of Apollo in Ian Hamilton Finlay's 'Gesamtkunstwerk' at Little Sparta, provides proof that there is truth in the legend that every year Apollo feels obliged to leave his Grecian world in Delphi and travel north-westwards towards the land beyond where the North Wind blows – the Hyperborean. That land can be found in the Hebridean world of Scotland and in Ireland's Atlantean islands. The Road to Meikle Seggie defines the journeys taken by all those who participated in the Demarco Gallery's Edinburgh Arts Summer School journeys towards these sea-girt landscapes on the extreme edge of Europe.

The Royal Scottish Academy, like the Royal Academy in London, came into being as a collective guild of artists. One of the main aims of the guild of artists was to find ways of supporting and promoting fellow artists and architects who were at the beginning of their careers. For this reason, for over 30 years, the Royal Scottish Academy presented an annual students' 'Open' exhibition. Since 2009, the Royal Scottish Academy has transformed this exhibition into its New Contemporaries Exhibition involving artists selected by the Academicians. So we are fortunate to have an Academy independently run by artists. Therefore, the theme of my Gillies Lecture is inspired by my thoughts on artists helping other artists.

As such an artist who helped others, Sir William Gillies managed to wear three hats: as a hard-working painter, as Principal of Edinburgh College of Art and as an outstanding President of the Royal Scottish Academy. He inspired me, as he did many of my contemporaries, as a teacher and by his commitment to the student-run Edinburgh College of Art Sketch Club. This was particularly important to me in my role as curator of the Club's 1951 exhibition. William Gillies' assessment of the art works he found interesting could be regarded as the official acknowledgement of a student's professional career. I have every reason to believe that my professional career as an art gallery director began with my experience as the Sketch Club exhibition curator.

With my thoughts on William Gillies and Roland Penrose as artists helping other artists, I am naturally thinking of Willem Sandberg. It was he who inspired me to accept the challenge of the 1970s. Willem Sandberg gave me the best possible advice when I read his thoughts on the nature of art.

The relation between man and man
The relation between man and his environment
Far away and nearby
Changes constantly

Today quicker than ever

Living in the reality
Behind the façade of appearances
The great artist is the first
To sense these changing relations
He renders them visible, audible, palpable
Creates their expression

He assists us to discover what happens
To penetrate, to understand

The constantly changing forms of art
Cannot be measure
By existing standards
They grow by new rules of their own

Great art
Is deeply rooted in society
And cannot be judged at once
Because criteria are lacking

At best
A sense of direction
In which our community is developing
May guide us

The critic can place new art
Within its setting
The museum man has the duty
To show it
But neither of them can really judge
Although many do it

The art of the present
Cannot be deduced from past creations
But it may introduce us
To the society of today
If we are willing to listen

The difficulty for many is
That like the deaf and dumb
We have to listen with our eyes
And as ever
To understand with the heart

With these poetic words, Willem Sandberg contributed a memorable introduction to the catalogue of the historic exhibition which took place in Dublin in 1967, not in a gallery but in the Royal Dublin Society building, in the spacious interior, famous for housing the Royal Dublin Horse Show. He was entitled to make such a statement as a member of the jury which selected the artists represented in the exhibition entitled 'ROSC'.

'ROSC' is the Old Irish word for 'the poetry of vision'. No other language has such a word to describe the work of the visual artist. Two Dublin-based artists, Michael Scott and Cecil King, helped to select the jury which chose the 50 international artists. My abiding memory of that first ROSC exhibition was seeing the work of John Latham close to one of the nail works of Günther Uecker, and the fact that I learned, in conversation with Günther Uecker, that his sister was the widow of Yves Klein and that Yves Klein had been a student at Trinity College Dublin. It was in that conversation that I first knew that Düsseldorf had become a city attracting artists from all over Europe so that looking back, I can see that 'Strategy: Get Arts' came into existence from what I now regard as a historic encounter. He is one of the artists in the Royal Scottish Academy exhibition who, like Magdalena Abakanowicz and myself, is celebrating his 80th birthday this year.

Willem Sandberg was a good friend. He made his mark in the history of modern art by saving the treasures of the Stedelijk Museum in Amsterdam from the ravages of World War Two as the Stedelijk's Director. He inspired a significant number of artists who, like him, were heavily disguised artists who knew that the history of art is entirely dependent on the ways in which artists relate to each other. Willem Sandberg was much respected by like-minded gallery directors with whom I have had the privilege of collaborating. I am thinking of Pontus Hultén, Rsyzard Stanisławski, Johannes Cladders, Ted Hickey, Karl Ruhrberg, Harald Szeemann, Marijan Susovski, David Baxandall and Jim Ede. It could be said that they have all died since I first knew them in the '60s and '70s, but I know that is most probably only a rumour because the life and work of serious artists live on in the art of those they have inspired.

They prepared the way for those who are still alive, who like their predecessors, are essentially artists playing the role of gallery directors. I am thinking of Rudi Fuchs, Susanne Page, Peter Selz, David Silcox, Martyn Anglesea, Sandy Nairne, Jennifer Gough-Cooper, Declan McGonagle, Ian McKenzie Smith, and Chris Carrell. I am also thinking of the hard-working, practising artists who instinctively help promote the work of other artists. There are too many to list everyone, but I must mention Gabriella Cardazzo, John David Mooney, Sonia Rolak, and Zbigniew Makarewicz and, of course, my invaluable deputy, Terry Ann Newman, and the 25-year-old recent fine art graduate of Edinburgh College of Art, Becky Campbell, who has been helping Terry Newman.

I must also mention all those members of the Board of Directors of the Demarco Gallery, The Demarco European Art Foundation, The Demarco Archive Trust and The Demarco European Cultural Initiative. Without them and those who became patrons of the Demarco Gallery and Archive, I could not have carried out the work which has resulted in the Demarco Archive. I am thinking particularly of John Martin, Robert McDowell, Mary James, Andrew Elliott, Victor McDougall, Bert Davies, James Ferguson,

Jean Polwarth, John Haldane, Arthur Watson, Duncan McFarlane, Giuseppe Panza, Giuliano Gori, Arthur Sackler and Michael Spens. I add to this list the names of so-called art critics such as Cordelia Oliver, Dorothy Walker, Georg Jappe. It is rumoured that they, too, have died.

I consider them among the Communion of Souls whose presence can be felt now in this lecture theatre. They provide proof that 'art originates in the meeting of friends'. Patrick Reyntiens, who I first knew as a fellow student at Edinburgh College of Art 60 years ago, reminded me of that inescapable fact when he participated in the Demarco Gallery's experimental summer school during the 1973 Edinburgh Festival. He spoke of his work as a stained-glass artist collaborating with his friend, John Piper, in the making of the historic windows of Coventry Cathedral. He was part of a faculty which included Buckminster Fuller, George Melly, Stuart Hopps, Joseph Beuys, Tadeusz Kantor, Paul Neagu, Hugh MacDiarmid, Lord Ritchie Calder, Caroline Tisdall, Marina Abramović, Norman MacCaig, Margaret Tait, George Mackay Brown, George Oliver, Bill Beech, Richard England, Ian Hamilton Finlay, Lord Macleod of Fiunary and Frank Ashton-Gwatkin.

I must also add all those original board members of the Traverse Theatre Club, the Richard Demarco Gallery, The Demarco European Art Foundation, The Demarco East European Art Foundation, The Demarco Cultural Initiative, The Association of Friends of the Demarco Gallery, the Association of Friends of the Demarco Archive.

Prominently among them, I am thinking of: Vivian Gough-Cooper, Jim Haynes, John Calder, Jacky Marian, Tom Mitchell, Tom Craig, AC Davis, Duncan MacFarlane, James Ferguson, Mark Goldberg, Lord (Dawyck) Haig, David Baxandall, Douglas Hall, Victor MacDougall, Mary James, John OR Martin, Andrew Elliott, James Walker and Michael Gascoigne.

They had all come together in my view as friends with shared ideals, values and hopes for the future; all fully committed to using the language of all the arts.

The Edinburgh Arts' students included Mark Francis, Tina Brown, Jane Chisholm, Anne Goring, Clare Street, Richard Noyce, Charles Stephens and Sandy Nairne.

The gap between the students and the faculty became indistinguishable.

Joseph Beuys regarded 'everyone as artists' with his 'Twelve-Hour Lecture' extolling the virtues of Anarcharsis Cloots as someone whose concepts of freedom and democracy were taken to heart by the leaders of the French Revolution. As part of his 'Action', Beuys transformed three blackboards into a tri-partite sculpture. I am sad to say that these works, along with 11 other master works by Joseph Beuys, were not destined to belong to collections in Scotland. Only one master work was acquired by the National Gallery of Modern Art and I am pleased to see that it forms a centre piece in the room dedicated to Joseph Beuys.

These boards had been used to teach many generations of Melville College schoolboys. They were available because the College had just ended its history as one of Edinburgh's prestigious Merchant Company Schools to amalgamate with Daniel Stewart's College. Its premises had become vacant in Melville Street within walking distance of the Demarco Gallery in nearby Melville Crescent. This enabled the Gallery to transform itself literally into a university of all the arts for a period of six weeks, at the same time as the Gallery was making use of Edinburgh University's derelict property at Forrest Hill near to Greyfriars historic churchyard.

This was the site of Edinburgh's equivalent of London's Bedlam; hence its reputation as 'The Forrest Hill Poorhouse'. Within its walls, and under its leaking roof, Tadeusz Kantor's Cricot II Theatre company performed and Joseph Beuys made his 'Three Pots Action', and there met Jimmy Boyle for the first time on the one day that Jimmy Boyle was released from Barlinnie Prison in order to see for himself his own sculptures on exhibition as part of the Demarco Gallery's contribution to the official programme of the Edinburgh Festival.

The Royal Scottish Academy exhibition 'Ten Dialogues: Richard Demarco – Scotland and the European Avant-garde' makes many references to the ways in which both Melville College and the Forrest Hill Poorhouse provided the well-nigh ideal spaces for the Demarco Gallery's visual and performing arts Edinburgh Festival programmes. Consider how the exhibition of Marina Abramović is focused on her action in the Melville College gymnasium as part of a programme of actions by artists from the gallery of young Serbian artists in Belgrade. Alongside Marina Abramović action, there is that of Raša Todosijević. Joseph Beuys can be seen observing their actions, along with Tom Marioni, one of the leading performance artists from Los Angeles. One of the most remarkable results from the work of these Yugoslav artists in Edinburgh was that Joseph Beuys accepted their invitation to speak at their students' centre in Belgrade. That is a little known and under-valued fact in the career of Joseph Beuys.

It can also be said that, under the aegis of the Demarco Gallery's Edinburgh Arts programmes, Scottish artists such as David Mach were invited to exhibit in Eastern Europe. Wiesław Borowski invited David Mach to make one of his major sculptural installations in the Foksal Gallery in Warsaw. I also think of the official exhibition at the 1990 Venice Biennale and the Scottish Pavilion in the heart of the Giardini within site of the Italian and British Pavilions. This brought together David Mach's large-scale bonsai trees in relation to Kate Whiteford's drawing laid upon the Giardini's grass lawn leading to the platform upon which Arthur Watson linked the waters of the Venice Lagoon with those of the Scottish east coast harbours of the Buchan. He also was one of the Scottish artists who exhibited alongside Ainslie Yule and Paul Neagu in the Collegium Artisticum in Sarajevo in 1988.

Looking at Ainslie Yule's exhibition I think of how he and I have known each other since the '60s and how it is entirely due to him that I found myself involved in his world at Kingston University. I also think of his extraordinary sculpture 'Three Score Years and Ten' which added a Scottish dimension to the Venice Biennale in 1993.

I must now consider the fact that from the very beginning of its existence in 1966, the Demarco Gallery had been obliged to extend its physical reality beyond the walls of its three-storey Edinburgh New Town house in Melville Crescent.

For the 1967 Edinburgh Festival in collaboration with Edinburgh University's School of Extra-Mural Studies, it presented the Edinburgh 'Open Hundred' exhibition in the University's Hume Tower. This followed a groundbreaking exhibition from the collection of the Galleria Nazionale D'Arte Moderna in Rome.

In 1968, the Gallery presented its exhibition of contemporary

Canadian art in collaboration with the Canada Council at
the Edinburgh College of Art. This prepared the way for the
College providing the setting for the 1970 exhibition the Gallery
presented in collaboration with the Düsseldorf Kunsthalle with the
palindromic title 'Strategy: Get Arts'.

2010 marks the 40th anniversary of this seminal exhibition
which introduced the art of Günther Uecker, Joseph Beuys, Gerhard
Richter, Blinky Palermo, Daniel Spoerri, Robert Filliou, George
Brecht, André Tomkins and many Fluxus artists to Scotland.

Arthur Watson and Euan McArthur have been content to focus
on the avant-garde exhibitions which proved that Scotland, in the
'60s and '70s, was in fruitful dialogue with Romania, Poland and
the former Yugoslavia However, I am imagining that their work
will be incomplete without taking into account the dialogues which
followed, linking Scotland with Lithuania, Belarus, Estonia, Latvia,
Hungary and Czechoslovakia, and not forgetting Austria, France,
Italy, Spain, Portugal, Greece, Malta, The Netherlands, Belgium,
Denmark, Norway and Sweden.

These exhibitions have been inextricably linked to a performing
arts programme emphasising the Demarco Gallery's origins in Jim
Haynes' Paperback Bookshop which provided a miniscule theatre
and gallery space, and the Traverse Theatre Gallery as well as John
Calder's opera festival 'Ledlanet Nights'. This performing arts
programme thus formed an integral part of the work of the Gallery
since the early '60s, leading inevitably to the work of the Demarco
European Art Foundation since 1993.

I am obliged to remember highlights in the Demarco Gallery's
Edinburgh Festival theatre programmes, many made possible by
the financial support of the British Council and Visiting Arts. I
am thinking in particular of Nancy Meckler's Freehold Theatre
production of *Antigone* and Józef Szjana's *Replique* at Melville
Crescent, Mladen Materić's Tattoo Theatre productions from
Sarajevo in Blackfriars Church, the Estonian Youth Theatre
production of *Romeo and Juliet* and Yvette Boszik's Hungarian
dance productions at St Mary's School, and the outdoor
productions of Shakespeare's *Macbeth* on Inchcolm Island and
Ravenscraig Castle involving La Zattera di Babele theatre from
Rome, John Bett's Scottish theatre company and the Vitebsk State

Theatre, and the many hundreds of theatre productions at the
Demarco Roxy Art House in collaboration with Xela Batchelder's
American Rocket Festival Productions, particularly Jarosław Fret's
Polish Teatr ZAR from Wrocław. The unforgettable highlights of
the 2010 Edinburgh Festival were 'Kabaret Kantor' programme of
Kantor-inspired plays in collaboration with Rose Bruford College
and Caroline Wiseman's 'The Leonardo Question'.

The RSA 'Ten Dialogues' exhibition brings together six artists
from continental Europe: Marina Abramović, Magdalena
Abakanowicz, Tadeusz Kantor and Paul Neagu, Joseph Beuys and
Günther Uecker, in fruitful dialogue with four Scots, David Mach,
Alastair MacLennan, Rory McEwen and Ainslie Yule.

When I consider certain parts of the exhibition, and I look at
Paul Neagu's 'Nine Catalytic Stations', I immediately think of his
dialogue with Merilyn Smith, Margot Sandeman, Ainslie Yule
and Fred Stiven, and I think, too, of the impact of his teaching
upon such artists as Anthony Gormley and Anish Kapoor and of
his profound friendships with his fellow Romanian artists, Horia
Bernea and Ion Bitzan, and most importantly, I think of my dear
friend, Radu Varia, who, in 1971, had the unenviable task of being
my official guide in Romania and having to deal with the terrifying
problem of President Ceaușescu's decision to cancel the official
Edinburgh Festival exhibition that Radu and I had planned.

Looking at Rory McEwen's work and taking into account his
untimely death at the age of 50, I am thinking of how indebted
I am to him, not only as an extraordinary Scottish artist, but as
a key member of the board of directors of the Demarco Gallery.
I firmly believe that, had he lived as a member of my generation,
his role would have been as a force for good in the process of
internationalising the Scottish art world. When I see his work,
I think of his important role as a collaborator with Joseph Beuys on
the Moor of Rannoch.

Standing in the extraordinary room created by Alastair
MacLennan, I have the clearest recollection of how he contributed
to a Demarco exhibition at the National Theatre in London for
an international conference of the world's leading oncologists. His
contribution was in perfect harmony with those of Joseph Beuys,
Tadeusz Kantor, Paul Neagu and Helen Chadwick. I remember,

too, how his action at Edinburgh College of Art during the 1984 Edinburgh Festival caused him to be in dialogue with George Melly, and with the artists of the Galleria del Cavallino, the Robert Fraser Gallery and the Australian and New Zealand artists who together represented the nature of the 1980s international avant-gardism. I also remember Alastair on board *The Marques* sailing from Belfast to the Isle of Arran across the Irish Sea.

The gigantic metal sculptures of Magdalena Abakanowicz redefine completely my ideas of the Court of King Arthur, and immediately evoke memories of her contribution to the Polish exhibition 'Atelier 72' which tied the Demarco Gallery in Melville Crescent, as a house of art, to the spires of St Mary's Cathedral, as a house of prayer standing 600 yards distant at the end of Melville Street, with the most effective use of a four-inch diameter, red coloured umbilical cord made of rope.

The sight of Kantor's grand emballage with its enormous black cloth covering iconic sculptural objects created by Kantor for his three Cricot II Theatre productions for the 1972, '73 and '76 Edinburgh Festivals cause me to recall the sight of all the characters he created and the genius of his Cricot II actors, particularly Zofia Kalińska as the Princess Abenceraga, and Sandy Nairne's Cardinal Archbishop forever opening and closing a door.

Similarly, looking at the extraordinary wall-hung sculptural objects of Günther Uecker, I see him exploring the world of what he regarded as The Pictlandgarden on The Road to Meikle Seggie, leading to Colin Lindsay-McDougall's castle of Lunga, overlooking the Corryvreckan. I see him, too, beside the sign indicating the farmstead of Meikle Seggie.

Looking at the David Mach portrait of myself made of countless burnt matchsticks, I can see Dik Mehta with his Super 8 camera recording the moment when it was set alight, causing flames to shoot high into the air outside the front door of the Demarco Gallery in Blackfriars Street at the 1992 Edinburgh Festival.

Although each of the ten artists are exhibited in well-defined separate sections, the exhibition is so designed that I can see clearly how altogether they make a unique statement about how Scotland had a role to play in the development of the spirit of European avant-gardism.

This exhibition is related to the exhibition 'Richard Demarco: A Life in Pictures'. It reveals the role I have endeavoured to play since my schooldays at Holy Cross Academy and my art school days at Edinburgh College of Art to show how my work as a watercolourist and printmaker has enabled me to make manifest what I have come to define as 'The Road to Meikle Seggie'.

This road exists through townscapes and landscapes, symbolising the journeys made not only by myself in the company of artists, students and teachers representing all the aspects of the arts and the sciences linking Edinburgh and the entire history of the Edinburgh Festival with continental Europe but also with my Italo-Irish forebears who made the long and arduous journeys to live the life of immigrants in Scotland.

They followed in the footsteps of Roman Legionaries, Celtic and medieval pilgrims, saints and travelling scholars and those Scottish Enlightenment luminaries who felt obliged to make their versions of The Grand Tour.

My drawings, watercolours and prints define nodal points on The Road to Meikle Seggie in the traces left by all those travellers and explorers and those who took the risk of discovering unexplored territories. These traces are observable in the form of dry-stone walls, telegraph poles, wooden fencing and signposts, all delineating the direction the road is taking through the landscape. In townscape, the Road is shaped by small inhabitable spaces, featuring doorsteps, doorways, windows, rooftops, window ledges and lampposts, as well as paving stones, all preferably time-worn and weathered. The Road is inextricably linked to the presence of human figures who define the theatre of everyday life.

Both the RSA exhibitions are complementary to the one I have devised at Craigcrook Castle which I have entitled, using Joseph Beuys' words, 'New Beginnings are in the Offing'.

This exhibition underlines the fact that the Demarco Collection and Archive is about the future as well as the past. It suggests the possibilities of many more dialogues to be added to the ten which constitute the exhibition at the Royal Scottish Academy. Joseph Beuys set his sights on the 'Offing' – rather than on the horizon which is measurable and represents the limitations of what human eyes can see without taking into account the mysterious nature of what lies beyond the horizon.

Some of these artists have the instincts of seafarers who steer their course towards the Offing. They can obviously be placed on the right-hand-side of a line drawn by Tadeusz Kantor. This is Kantor's 'The Demarcation Line'. It came into being as his contribution to the Polish Edinburgh Festival exhibition 'Atelier 72'. I have a feeling that everyone who truly comprehends the significance of this RSA exhibition will realise that their own version of The Road to Meikle Seggie will place them in the company of Kantor and his Cricot II Theatre on the right-hand-side of the Demarcation Line, among the few who have escaped the highly questionable theories of post-modernism.

Arthur Watson and Euan McArthur have been working at the University of Dundee since 2005 on the digitisation process of the Archive with the help of the Arts and Humanities Research Council's generous grant. Now, as curators of the 'Ten Dialogues' exhibition, they have extended this work, in collaboration with Colin Greenslade and his colleagues at the Royal Scottish Academy and aided by Ann Simpson and her team at the National Gallery of Modern Art. I am indebted to all of them, and also to Bill Scott and Ian Howard, and all the Academicians who have shown their willingness to support an exhibition which amplifies the essential nature of the Demarco Collection and Archive. I am also indebted to my deputy, Terry Ann Newman, whose unflagging work has enabled the director of both the Demarco European Art Foundation and the Demarco Archive Trust to commit themselves to ensuring the fact that at Craigcrook Castle an exhibition could be installed as a complementary statement to 'Ten Dialogues'.

Finally, I cannot forget Joseph Beuys' definition of art – '*Kunst ist Kapital*' – which, of course, does not translate into English as 'Art is Capital'. Art is not about money. '*Le mot juste*' is surely 'wealth' originating in the word 'health'. It signifies wellbeing and the common good. Joseph Beuys is thus sending us a 40-year-old message which we must surely take seriously when they want to use the word 'wellbeing' to define the state of mind of the electorate.

This lecture deliberately took the form of a historical survey to establish the fact that the Demarco Collection and Archive is

a total art work which has come into being over six decades as
a result of the contributions made to it by generations of artists,
all inspired by the physical reality of Scotland, its history and
its cultural heritage. I sincerely hope that this will surely cast a
light on the undoubted complex nature of the genesis of the 'Ten
Dialogues' exhibition. I am grateful that I can regard it as the latest
development in an ongoing, living work of art.

Bibliography

Arcari, Virginia, *Picinisco – Uncovering 1,000 years of History*, Virginia Arcari, 2017

Astaire, Lesley and Martine, Roddy, *Living in Scotland*, with photographs by Fritz von der Schulenberg, Thames & Hudson, 1997

Astaire, Lesley and Martine, Roddy, *Living in the Highlands*, with photographs by Eric Ellington, Thames & Hudson, 2000

Bellman, David (ed), *A Journey from Hagar Qim to the Ring of Brodgar* with an introduction by Lucy Lippard; *Notes for a Descriptive Phenomenology* with an introductory essay from David Bellman

Beuys Kantor Demarco , MOCAK (The Museum of Contemporary Art), Krakow, 2015 (In English and in Polish with a foreword by Maria Anna Potocka)

Birrell, Ross and Finlay, Alec (eds), *Justified Sinners: An Archaeology of Scottish Counter-Culture 1960–2000*, Pocket Books (Polygon Press), 2002

Boswell, James. *Tour to the Hebrides* (from original manuscript) Ralph. H. Isham, 1936

Boyle, Jimmy, *A Sense of Freedom*, Pan Books, 1985

Boyle, Jimmy, *The Pain of Confinement*, Pan Books, 1985

Bruce, George, *Festival in the North: The Story of the Edinburgh Festival*, Robert Hale, 1975

Carlin, Norah (ed), *Holy Cross Academy: The Life and Times of a Catholic School 1907–1969*, illustrated with drawings by Richard Demarco, New Cut Press, 2009

Collins, Hugh, *Autobiography of a Murderer*, Macmillan, 1997

Collins, Hugh, *Walking Away*, Rebel Inc., 2001

Crawford, Iain, *Banquo on Thursdays: The Inside Story of 50 Years of the Edinburgh Festival*, Goblinshead, 1997

Dally, Jenny and Jacob, Mary Jane (eds), *Magdalena Abakanowicz: Writings and Conversations*, Abakanowicz Arts and Cultural Foundation, Skira Editore, 2022

Demarco, Richard, *Artysta Jako Odktywca* with a foreword by Krzysztof Noworyta. Published in Wroclaw in Polish Language by the Depot Gallery.

Demarco, Richard, *A Life in Picture*, Northern Books, 1978

Demarco, Richard, *Droga Do Meikle Seggie* with a foreword by Thomas Wilson. Published in Wroclaw in Polish language by the Depot Gallery.

Demarco, Richard, *The Road to Meikle Seggie,* with a foreword by Stefania Del Bravo and an essay by Donald Smith – 'The Road Goes On', Luath Press, 2015.

Demarco, Richard, *The Italian Connection* edited by Laura Leuzzi, Elaine Shemilt and Stephen Partridge, John Libbey Press

Dudley Edwards, Owen, *City of a Thousand Worlds: Edinburgh in Festival*, Mainstream, 1991

Exhibition Catalogue: Demarco European Art Foundation Exhibition of Maritime Art 'A Festival of Sea' at Leith Docks. Demarco European Art Foundation in collaboration with Forth Ports PLC, Aberdeen Assets Management and Giclee UK and the archive of James and Pamela Currie.

Exhibition Catalogue of *Bougé*. Presented by The Richard Demarco Gallery as part of the Official Exhibition Programme of the Edinburgh Festival 1984 in collaboration with the Ministry of Culture in Paris, Institut Français d'Écosse in Edinburgh, Musée des Beaux Arts, Beune Centre D'Action Culturelle, Monbeliaro with an introduction by Andre Laude 'Tu Boiges, Tu Vis, Je Vois.' Curated by Georges Daldachino.

Gordon Bowe, Nicola and Cumming, Elizabeth (eds), *The Arts and Crafts Movements in Dublin & Edinburgh 1885–1925*, Irish Academy Press, 1998

Henderson Scott, Paul (ed), *Spirits of the Age: Scottish Self Portraits*, Saltire Society, 2005

Hogg, Brian, *Cosmopolitan Scum! Edinburgh, The Arts and the Counter Culture*, Nove Mob (Ink) Publishing, 2019

MacArthur, Euan and Watson, Arthur (eds), *Ten Dialogues: Richard Demarco, Scotland and the European Avant Garde*, Royal Scottish Academy, 2010

Martell JF, *Reclaiming Art in the Age of Artifice: A treatise, critique, and a call to action*, Evolver Editions, North Atlantic Books, 2015

Martin, Marilyn (ed), *Kevin Atkinson: Art and Life*, The Kevin Patricia Atkinson Trust and Print Matters Heritage, 2022

Martin, John OR (ed), *The Demarco Collection and Archive: An Introduction*, Demarco Archive Trust

Martine, Roddy, *Scottish Clan & Family Names: Their Arms, Origins & Tartans*. First published Bartholemew in 1987. Foreword by Sir Malcolm Innes of Edingight.

Martine, Roddy, *Edinburgh Military Tattoo*, Robert Hale, 2001

Martine, Roddy, *Scotland: The Land and the Whisky*, John Murray 1994.

Martine, Roddy, *Scorpion on the Ceiling: A Scottish Colonial Family in South East Asia*, Librario, 2004

Martine, Roddy, *Secrets of Rosslyn*, Birlinn, 2006.

Maxwell Stuart, Flora, *A Gift of Time: A Memoir*, Birlinn, 2004.

Martine, Roddy, *This Too Shall Pass: Reminiscences of East Lothian*, Birlinn, 2009

Montgomery, Bryan, *Pictures for an exhibition: Works Collected by Bryan Montgomery during the past 30 years*, The Richard Demarco Gallery in collaboration with SITE (Scottish International Trade Exhibitions Limited) and Andy Montgomery Ltd, 2021 Mooney, David John, *Vatican Observatory and the Arts: The Sculpture of John David Mooney at Castel Gandolfo*, University of Notre Dame Press, 1999

Mooney, David John, *Vatican Observatory and the Arts: The Sculpture of John David Mooney at Castel Gandolfo*, University of Notre Dame Press, 1999.

Murawska-Muthesius, Katarzyna and Zarzecka, Natalia (eds), *Kantor was Here: Tadeusz Kantor in Great Britain*, Black Dog Publishing, 2011

Nasmyth, Charles (ed), *Hamish Henderson A Conversation Piece: A Portrait in Six Conversations*, Fife Global Press, 2022

Pollock, David, *Edinburgh's Festivals: A Biography*, Luath Press, 2023

Royle, Trevor, *A Diary of Edinburgh*, with pen drawing illustrations by Richard Demarco, Polygon Books, 1981

Scollard OSB, Sister Anselma, *Art, Truth and Time: Essays on Art*, with a foreword by Richard Demarco, Luath Press, 2019

Sheeler, Jessie, *Little Sparta: The Garden of Ian Hamilton Finlay*, with photographs by Andrew Lawson, Francis Lincoln, 2003

Spens, Michael and Janet Mackenzie (eds), *Studio International* Special issue, Vol. 207, No. 1,030

Stanley, Tim, *Whatever Happened to Tradition? History, Belonging and the Future of the West*, Bloomsbury Continuum, 2021

Swan, Douglas, *Ein Moderner Klassiker (A Modern Classic)*, ed. by Axel Wendelburger, Museum August Macke Haus, Encounters Hans-Bonn Exhibition, 2020

Tisdall, Caroline, *Joseph Beuys: Bits and Pieces*, with an introduction by Caroline Tisdall and Richard Demarco, Richard Demarco Gallery in association with the Arnolfini Gallery, Bristol and Red Lion House, 1987

Watson, Arthur (ed), *Richard Demarco 2020*, Demarco Archive Trust and Duncan of Jordanstone College of Art, 2021

Weikop, Christian, 'Anselm Kiefer's Occupations through a Glass Darkly', *Studies in Photography: Understanding the Past,* ed. by Alexander Hamilton, Scottish Society for the display of Photography, 2021

Weikop, Christian, *Strategy: Get Arts: 35* 'Artists Who Broke the Rules', *Studies in Photography*, 2021.

Watson, Arthur (ed), *Richard Demarco 2020*, Demarco Archive Trust and Duncan of Jordanstone College of Art

A Survey of History, an essay by Frank Ashton-Gwatkin Inspired by EDINBURGH ARTS. Edited by David Bellman. Research and Art Work by Jeanne Sanschargrin and Carol Swift. Caledonian Press. Published by Richard Demarco Gallery 1976

Index of Names and Places

Luath Press Limited

committed to publishing well written books worth reading

LUATH PRESS takes its name from Robert Burns, whose little collie Luath (*Gael.*, swift or nimble) tripped up Jean Armour at a wedding and gave him the chance to speak to the woman who was to be his wife and the abiding love of his life. Burns called one of the 'Twa Dogs' Luath after Cuchullin's hunting dog in Ossian's *Fingal*. Luath Press was established in 1981 in the heart of Burns country, and is now based a few steps up the road from Burns' first lodgings on Edinburgh's Royal Mile. Luath offers you distinctive writing with a hint of unexpected pleasures.

Most bookshops in the UK, the US, Canada, Australia, New Zealand and parts of Europe, either carry our books in stock or can order them for you. To order direct from us, please send a £sterling cheque, postal order, international money order or your credit card details (number, address of cardholder and expiry date) to us at the address below. Please add post and packing as follows: UK – £1.00 per delivery address; overseas surface mail – £2.50 per delivery address; overseas airmail – £3.50 for the first book to each delivery address, plus £1.00 for each additional book by airmail to the same address. If your order is a gift, we will happily enclose your card or message at no extra charge.

Luath Press Limited
543/2 Castlehill
The Royal Mile
Edinburgh EH1 2ND
Scotland
Telephone: 0131 225 4326 (24 hours)
Email: sales@luath.co.uk
Website: www.luath.co.uk